Why You Should Read This Book and How Other Holistic Practitioners and Coaches Have Benefited From What's In It

"Working with Jesse and Sharla completely transformed my business. When I met them, I didn't know business or marketing and I hated sales and was only making $45,000 per year in my nutrition practice. I never took time off because I was afraid I would miss new clients. **NOW I EARN $250,000 PER YEAR, I'M BOOKED OUT MONTHS IN ADVANCE.** I'm so grateful for what I've learned and recommend that every Holistic Practitioner and Coach learn the skills Jesse and Sharla teach."
-Rose Cole, Holistic Nutrition Coach and founder of www.Wellness with Rose.com

"Using Heartselling™ I serve my clients in a way they have not experienced before. I listen to them and…we share a deep connection. They see my program as the answer they have been looking for. The natural next step is for them to sign up. **Only 6 months ago,** the paint was literally still drying on the walls of my Wellness and Detox Spa….now I **HAVE OVER 420 CLIENTS.** On the first day using Heartselling™, I **SOLD OVER $8,500.00 OF PROGRAMS! I NOW HAVE OVER A 90% SALES CONVERSION RATE AND HAVE DOUBLED THE OVERALL SALES REVENUE OF MY BUSINESS IN THE LAST 6 MONTHS,** thanks to the Heartselling™ model! I am so thankful to Sharla, Jesse and the entire Rejuvenate Team! You have totally changed my life!"
-Shannon Law, The Detox Diva, Detox Coach, Colon Hydrotherapist, and founder of Radiance Health Solutions

"Since I started working with Jesse Koren and Sharla Jacobs only 15 months ago, **I'VE MADE OVER $130,000 IN A BRAND NEW BUSINESS**…and this is just the beginning. Thank you Rejuvenate."
-PJ Van Hulle, Prosperity ⌐ 　　　　　　　　　 Incorporated

"Jesse Koren and Sharla Jacobs made a huge difference in my life. It's like being handed a map that I should have had years ago! **I DOUBLED AND THEN TRIPLED MY PRACTICE.** Thank you for your wisdom, support, acknowledgment and skill building. **Your program should be offered to all graduating holistic practitioners.** "
-Abby Caplin, MD, MA Mind-Body Medicine Counseling

"Jesse Koren and Sharla Jacobs made it so easy and fun to have conversations to promote my business. **I GOT 50 NEW CLIENTS IN 90 DAYS.**"
-Talya Lutzker, Ayurvedic Practitioner and founder of Talya's Kitchen

"Jesse Koren and Sharla Jacobs helped me make calls and have conversations much more easily and frequently. **I INCREASED MY CLIENT BASE BY 300%.**"
-Shannon McGinnis, Professional Organizer, founder of Organized 4 Success and author of *10-Minute Tidy*

"When I started working with Jesse and Sharla, I was seeing 15 clients per week. **AFTER 90 DAYS, I SEE AN AVERAGE OF 39 CLIENTS PER WEEK.**"
-Cristina Clifford, L.Ac.

"Before working with Jesse and Sharla, I used to sit in my office and hope clients would miraculously come to me by referrals. I learned so much that I went from a 12' x 12' office and $1,800 per month to an office with four treatment rooms and between **$8,000-9,000 PER MONTH IN INCOME.**"
-Cammi Montieth, ND

"Using the tools I learned from Jesse and Sharla **I MADE OVER $40,000 IN ONE WEEKEND.** The miracles are too many to list but they have allowed my financial and Spiritual life to…magnify in abundance. Thank you!"
-Dr. Laurie Moore, The Miracle Worker, Animal Intuitive

SELL IS NOT A 4-LETTER WORD

How to Serve More Clients and Create a 6-Figure Practice

Jesse Koren and Sharla Jacobs

First Edition

Rejuvenate Training, Inc. • Santa Cruz, CA

Sell is Not a 4-Letter Word
How to Serve More Clients and Create a 6-Figure Practice
By Jesse Koren and Sharla Jacobs

Published by
Rejuvenate Training, Inc.
1729 Seabright Ave., Suite C
Santa Cruz, CA 95062 USA
1-800-632-2944
Info@RejuvenateTraining.com
http://www.RejuvenateTraining.com

ISBN: 978-0-9821388-0-9

Cover design by Bigfish Smallpond Design

REJUVENATE YOUR PRACTICE
2 DAY INTENSIVE
CERTIFICATE

Jesse Koren, Sharla Jacobs and Rejuvenate

Training invite you and a friend to attend

the Rejuvenate Your Practice 2 Day Intensive,

as complimentary guests. To register

and for more information go to

www.RYPScholarship.com

If you have no access to a computer,

call toll-free **1-800-632-2944 x100**

Claim Your **Full Scholarship** to the Rejuvenate Your Practice
2 Day Intensive www.RYPScholarship.com

Dedication

This book is dedicated to Jacob Koren, our first child five months of age at the time of this book's first publication. In raising consciousness and helping people to become more successful through Heartselling™, it is our intention to create a better world for you to grow and thrive.

Acknowledgments

This book would not have been possible without the support and encouragement of so many people. First, we would like to thank The Great Spirit for continually guiding us to take risks and to support more people through our work. Second, we would like to thank our parents Barry Koren, Felice Bassuk, Standley Jacobs, and Bonnie Moon for your unwavering love and support in all that we do. Next, we would like to thank our many clients over the years. You have inspired us to keep teaching this system, because we have seen the incredible results you've produced in such a short period of time. We've watched your clientele expand, and with it, the amount of good you do in the world. Thank you for proving to us again and again that Heartselling™ is a powerful system.

We are grateful for our many coaches and mentors who paved the path for our business success.

A special thanks goes to all the members of our team over the years who contributed greatly to the growth of Rejuvenate Training, especially Johanna Thorn, Sylvia Valentine, Sonali Chapron, Jen Aly, Michelle Gronen, Diana Morgan, Carol Daly, Taj Leahy, Michelle Melendez, Sarah Medlicott, Corey Hale, Angela Lindsay, Laura Rice, Rick Hindman, Lisa Scott, Warren Angelo, Michele Campbell, Rebecca Cowan, Fani Nicheva, and Bob von Elgg. We couldn't have done it without you.

About the Authors

Award-winning 6 figure coaches Jesse Koren and Sharla Jacobs teach Holistic Practitioners and Coaches how to earn 6 figures in their business without compromising their values. They are the co-founders of Rejuvenate™ Training, the home of the Rejuvenate Your Practice 2 Day Intensive.

Rejuvenate™ Training's workshops and training programs have helped thousands and thousands of Practitioners and Coaches increase their business success. Jesse and Sharla are the authors of seven information products, including **"The Complete Heartselling**™ **(not hard-selling) System"** and the developers of seven training programs. They teach Practitioners and Coaches how to help more people by successfully marketing their business, leading lucrative workshops, and creating and leading their team to **double, triple, and even quadruple their income.**

They are interviewed in the best-selling book, "Who do you think you are?" along with transformational leaders such as Dr. Bob Proctor, Jack Canfield, and Joe Vitale.

They live in Santa Cruz, California, with their son Jacob and their cat Destri.

Jesse and Sharla can be reached via their website at **www.RejuvenateTraining.com**.

Preface: A Note from Jesse and Sharla

Dear Holistic Practitioner or Coach,

We know what it's like to want to make a real difference in people's lives and not be able to get enough clients. The good news is that you no longer have to feel that way. By reading this book, you'll learn the essential keys to easily and effortlessly attract more clients.

There are many other sales training books. But we want to congratulate you on choosing this book, because it shows that you want to get more clients without compromising your values. Your choice shows that you want your "sales conversations" to reflect the integrity and heart of your business. It's our greatest privilege to show you how to do that.

In this book we'll teach you how to have Heartselling™ (not hard-selling) conversations to attract all the clients you desire. You will learn how to leave your potential clients feeling better than you found them, and many of them will sign up for your services.

Thank you for your commitment to serving more people through your practice. Right now, there are people waiting for you. Their lives will be happier because you were willing to read this book and practice Heartselling™ in your everyday life. And with every new client you take on, the world becomes a safer, more loving place.

Happy Heartselling™,

Jesse & Sharla

Jesse Koren and Sharla Jacobs

Contents

Claim Your **Full Scholarship** to the Rejuvenate Your Practice
2 Day Intensive www.RYPScholarship.com

PART I
Heartselling™ Basics to Attract More Clients

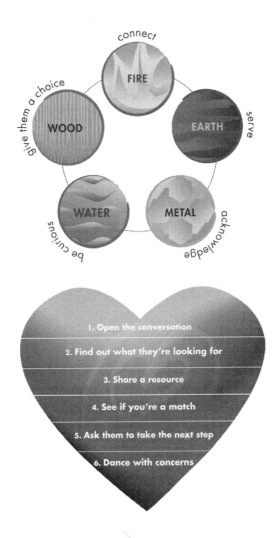

1

The New Model of Selling:
Why "S-E-L-L" is Not a 4-Letter Word

There you are at the used car lot and you can feel him lurking. You need a car but you're not really finding "your" car in this lot. But here he comes sauntering toward you. Intuitively, you start walking toward the exit, but his pace quickens and he intercepts you. He looks at you like a coyote, ready to sink his teeth into "the sale."

He shakes your hand and flashes you his bright shiny smile. He starts telling you why this car would be perfect for you and how good you would look inside it. But all you want is to get out of the car lot. You've been "sold" before and you're not going to let it happen again.

Finally, he takes a breath, and you use that brief moment to tell him that you are late for an appointment. He tries to keep you there, but you are insistent. You leave the lot with a feeling of relief mixed with a sick feeling in the pit of your stomach...

Another terrible sales experience.

Perhaps you've had an experience like this at a used car lot. We have. If not there, our guess is that you've had that sick feeling at the pit of your stomach at some point in your life when someone tried to sell you something.

Why? Because the old paradigm of selling was about manipulation and domination. It was about handling objections and closing sales. It used sales tactics and gimmicks and turned people into numbers. The object was to sell people stuff, regardless of whether it would benefit them or not.

It's no wonder that so many practitioners and coaches think "SELL" is a 4-letter word.

Yet if you want to be successful in your practice, you've got to learn how to sell.

So how do you sell your services without compromising your values? And how can you learn how to sell in a way that honors your potential client and creates true connection between the two of you?

This is what you're about to learn in this book.

You see, we've discovered that selling can be the most heartfelt, spiritual thing you can do for another human being.

You can have really heartfelt conversations where your potential clients practically talk themselves into working with you. And this is not some manipulative technique or gimmick. It's the authentic and natural way to support your potential clients to get what they truly want. We call it "Heartselling™."

When you use Heartselling™ (not hard selling), you completely shift the focus of the conversation from your services to your potential client's needs. You ask questions to discover more about them and what they're looking for. And you support them to get what they want.

Note from Sharla: At every Rejuvenate Your Practice 2 Day Intensive we do a live Heartselling™ demonstration* with a participant. At an intensive in Santa Cruz, I asked for a volunteer and was immediately drawn to work with a beautiful, vibrant woman with short red hair and exotic clothes named Jan.

As she approached the stage, I realized we had met before at a workshop, so that's how we started the conversation. During the course of the Heartselling™ conversation, I discovered she had a vision to help a LOT of people by leading retreats. I could see her inspiration…and I could also see her frustration

*You can read the transcript of this Heartselling™ conversation in Chapter 17
**Learn more about Jan at www.TantricJoy.com

with not having the next steps to see her vision come to life.

First we uncovered what "a LOT of people" really meant and I supported her to feel what it would be like to have this dream come true. And she opened and then opened some more. It was like witnessing a flower blooming.

And then I shared with her that we had a step-by-step system to help her earn tens of thousands of dollars leading her retreats…and she opened even more. By the time we were done with the Heartselling™ conversation, she was in tears of joy at the excitement of what was possible for her and for her clients to come. By the end of the workshop, she said Yes to herself by signing up for the programs that will help her achieve this dream.

Only three months after signing up for our programs, Jan not only filled one of her workshops but had a waiting list. She is on her way to creating the success we discussed during our initial Heartselling™ conversation.

It is Heartselling™ conversations like these that remind us why we love selling. Yes, we really said *"We love selling."* Because when we have a Heartselling™ conversation with a potential client, we know their life will never be the same. They will see a new possibility for their life. Or rekindle an old dream that they may have given up on.

Heartselling™ is about opening them to deeper parts of themselves and having them say Yes to what their higher self wants for them.

The biggest difference between hard selling and Heartselling™ is that hard sellers talk a lot, whereas Heartsellers™ ask a lot of questions. The experience is that your potential client is actually talking themselves into your services.

This is what makes Heartselling™ so powerful and has you become a magnet for the clients who will most benefit from your services.

2

Why Heartselling™ is Essential to Your Business Success

We've spoken with thousands of Holistic Practitioners and Coaches and we've found one common theme:

Most are struggling to get clients.

Unfortunately, many fall prey to the myth that if they just get "good enough" at what they do, clients will come to them. So, they go back to school for advanced trainings, or start adding another modality to their repertoire. And another, and another, and another. After spending thousands or tens of thousands of dollars getting trained in their modalities, many still don't have the clients they need to make ends meet.

Some will focus on the Law of Attraction to bring them clients. They visualize clients coming, meditate on them coming, and pray for them to come.

They will talk to everyone except their potential clients about their services. Anything to avoid sales conversations. Why? Because they don't want to be seen as pushy, manipulative, or obnoxious, like the used car salesman we shared about earlier.

So, they print up flyers and brochures and buy expensive ads in newspapers. They end up spending a lot of money and getting really frustrated.

Why? Because the days are gone when there is one medicine man or medicine woman in every village. There are a growing number of new practitioners and coaches that start up their practice every day.

And with so many Holistic Practitioners and Coaches to choose from, most people would rather work with someone they know and trust than with someone they see in a print advertisement or find on the internet. Or they'd rather get a referral from someone they trust than work with a complete stranger.

So, while advertising is one way of getting known, if you rely on it exclusively to fill your practice, you're fighting a losing battle.

And even if you do get some calls from your print or internet advertising, when you pick up the phone or return those calls, you will still have to have a sales conversation before they sign up for your services.

So, selling is the most important skill you can learn when it comes to sustaining your practice. But if you're going to learn to sell, we'd rather you learn the art of Heartselling™ than hard-selling techniques.

This book is called "Sell is Not a 4-Letter Word." So what does that mean?

Sell is usually spelled: "S-E-L-L"

But we have a different perspective about selling. Cross out the two L's and replace them with three letters: R-V-E

When you practice Heartselling™, instead of hard-selling, you are serving. Hard-selling is trying to convince potential clients that they need what you have. In Heartselling™, you find out

what they need and offer your services as a way of serving them.

This is why "Sell" is not really a 4-letter word…it's actually a 5-letter word and doesn't need to be associated with profanity☺.

Heartselling™ is the art of turning a selling conversation into a healing conversation. So, rather than selling something *to* someone, you are working with them to discover what will most serve them.

When you're nervous or uncomfortable about selling your services, it might be because you're missing the primary ingredient in any Heartselling™ conversation: service.

In this book, we'll teach you how to take the focus off yourself and put it on serving your potential client, just like in the example above with Jan. When you learn how to do this, your confidence in yourself and your services will grow, and you'll discover that Heartselling™ is a natural extension of who you are.

In fact, you will find that when you let your fears stop you from offering your services, you will feel like you are selling out on your potential client. It will feel like robbing them of having their best life.

In this book, you're going to learn how to turn those dreaded sales conversations into Heartselling™ conversations. So that more people say Yes to you and feel supported, inspired, and compelled to take the next steps.

Once you become a master Heartseller™, you'll be successful at whatever you choose to do in life and you'll be able to attract as many clients as you want into your business.

And once you learn the basics of Heartselling™ in Part I, we'll share some of our favorite leveraged strategies for earning 6 figures in Part II of this book.

3

How Heartselling™
Changed Our Lives

If you've avoided selling up to this point, we understand why. You might think that people who are great at selling were born that way. At one time we felt the same way. And while it's true that some people have a natural aptitude for selling, anyone can learn to be an amazing Heartseller™.

Note from Sharla: I discovered Heartselling™ out of the pain of not being able to make a living as a licensed acupuncturist and life coach.

I entered the field of acupuncture because I fell in love with the model of the Five Elements. I was also told that acupuncture was a booming field. So I thought I would have no problem making a living at it. After a Master's program of 3 years, a grueling board exam, and a coaching certification program during the last 6 months of my Master's program, I was so excited to start making the difference that I had been dreaming about, and I expected masses of people to flock to me for my transformational acupuncture and coaching services.

But I was wrong.

I discovered that I still had a lot of work to do in order to receive money for my services and feel good about myself as a professional. And it wasn't until I really put myself out there to try to get clients that I discovered how painful it was to want to serve people so badly but not be able to share about what I did in an attractive enough way that people would pay me for it. It didn't take long to realize that, with $80,000 in debt from *acupuncture school, I was in trouble. Because I wasn't earning enough money in my business, my debt was rapidly increasing. So, after a few months of struggling to make it in my business, I cancelled my gym membership and cut all my other "extra" expenses. I remember being at the grocery store one day and thinking that I must stop eating organic food because I couldn't afford it anymore.*

It was such a confusing time for me because I wanted to help people; I just didn't know how to get clients. I was scared and thinking, "How am I going to get people to pay me for my services and help them improve their life when I can't even take care of myself?"

But, I had attended a seminar where I realized that no matter what problems I had, there were people out there who had gone through the same problems and had overcome them...and the key was to find these people and learn from them.

I had a friend who was a coach and mentor to people who were new in business. He promised that if I worked with him, I would triple my income in three months. At the time I wasn't making much, just over $20,000 a year, but it meant if I was successful I would earn $60,000 a year, and I thought that was a good place to start. I knew if I could get to $60,000, I could do a lot more.

The only way he would work with me was if I promised to do my homework. I didn't know what the homework would be and I didn't have the money to hire him (at $600 per month), but he said that I would triple my income in 3 months!

So I borrowed the money from Jesse and signed up for his business coaching program. When he assigned me homework, I almost fell off my seat—can you guess what it was?

My homework was to have 20 business conversations, 5 days a week. That's 100 sales conversations per week!

Both scared and excited, I had made a no-matter-what decision and there was no turning back. I was going to give this everything (and I had borrowed the money from Jesse to pay for it, so I couldn't let him down). And after all, I couldn't go back to having a J-O-B.

I've found there are no accidents. Because of the sheer number of conversations I had during those few months (true confession: I really averaged about 12 conversations a day), I started to understand what works and what doesn't work in sales conversations because I took the time to evaluate each conversation.

And it was during those 3 months that Jesse and I had the "Divine Download" of what was the beginning of the Heartselling™ model you're about to learn in this book.

It was like receiving a treasure map! And within 3 months, I tripled my practice, just as my coach promised.

When other practitioners, coaches, and friends saw this, they wanted to know how I was doing it. Jesse and I started sharing with people and they were so excited that we created our first CD set, which eventually led to the Rejuvenate Your Practice 2 Day Intensive.

Note from Jesse: While Sharla was going through acupuncture school, I was training to be a coach. When I was a teenager, I got very depressed and after years of personal growth workshops and counseling sessions, I was ready to take all the gifts I'd received and pay them forward.

Claim Your **Full Scholarship** to the Rejuvenate Your Practice
2 Day Intensive www.RYPScholarship.com

When I got out of coaching training, I did what most Holistic Practitioners and Coaches do, which is pass out business cards and hang flyers all over town.

I expected my phone to start ringing. It didn't. So, I waited patiently.

I waited and waited and waited and waited and waited and waited...

Until one day, the phone rang. And it was my mom asking me when I was going to get a job.

So you know the people who stand outside of the grocery store trying to sell you coupon books? I decided to do that. I got my clipboard, my sales script, and I was ready to go.

Lots of people said no to me, and some people even walked into doors trying to avoid me.

At first I hated the rejection and I was terrible at selling coupon books... until I discovered Heartselling™ principle #1. When I keep my heart open, more people say yes to me.

Soon after, I became one of the hottest coupon book sellers around.

Then, one day, I found out that although my sales script said that 50% of the sales were donated to charity, it was a total lie. That day, I hardly sold any coupon books, and I discovered Heartselling™ Principle #2: I can't sell something that I can't stand behind. So I quit.

And proceeded to get another job, and another job. And another...

Eight jobs later, I'd all but given up on my dream of helping lots of people... if it wasn't for Sharla, I might have.

I watched Sharla graduate from Acupuncture School, flounder for a few months, hire a coach, and then within 3 months, triple her practice.

I would cringe when I listened to many of her "sales" conversations. Afterward, I would ask, "Hunny, do you think maybe you were being a little pushy?"

After 3 months, I noticed that she had become masterful at having in her conversations. Listening to her was so inspiring, in fact, that we discovered Heartselling™ Principle #3. Whether they become your client or not, always leave people in a better place.

And Sharla did. She became so heartfelt in her conversations with potential clients, that 90 days later, she had MORE THAN tripled her practice.

She was ecstatic. And even though I was happy that she paid me back, I found myself picking fights with her almost every night. I was secretly very jealous. She was thriving and it felt like she was leaving me behind.

So, armed with my new Heartselling™ tools, I decided to give it one more shot. I decided to do whatever it took to get my coaching business to take off.

I hired a coach, and instead of going to personal growth workshops I started getting business training.

I set out to have 2-3 Heartselling™ conversations per day. In one month I attracted enough clients to give 30 days notice to my job. And I haven't looked back since. Soon after, I knew I had mastered Heartselling™ because I brought in 16 clients in one month.

Together, we developed the Heartselling™ model into the powerful client magnet tool it is today. Our business grew quickly, to the point that it has now become a movement. We feel so blessed to teach the world's most heartfelt people (YOU!) how to earn 6 figures in your business while staying true to your values.

Years ago, getting a job was our security. Now, Heartselling™ is our security. We know that we can move to any city in the US and create a thriving practice within 1-3 months.

Many of our clients now have that security as well. And we wrote this book so that you, too, can have that kind of security.

We wouldn't have been able to accomplish any of this without shifting how we think about selling. As we said earlier, Heartselling™ teaches you to take the focus off yourself and put it on serving your potential clients. When you learn how to do this, you'll find yourself feeling completely confident in conversations with them. And, if you believe that your services can change someone's life for the better but you don't let them know about it, then you are doing them a *disservice*. This is why it is imperative that you learn Heartselling™.

4

The 5 Elements of Heartselling™

When you master the 5 Elements of Heartselling™, you've got a heart-centered formula to have amazing conversations with potential clients and to quickly increase your income.

The 5 Elements are the foundation of Heartselling™. And what makes Heartselling™ different from any other sales training out there is that it is a holistic model. It isn't full of techniques and gimmicks. It's about using your intuition and becoming a client magnet.

So what are the 5 Elements? We'll discuss them in depth in the next five chapters, but let's take a moment for a brief overview.

The 5 Elements of Heartselling™

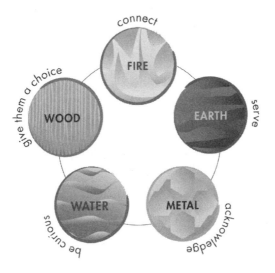

The Fire Element is about connection. Imagine the warmth, laughter, and coziness you feel when you sit around a campfire. Before engaging in any Heartselling™ conversation you must authentically connect from your heart with your potential client.

The Earth Element is about service. When you are in the energy of the Earth Element, you feel as abundant as the planet Earth, and from this feeling of abundance you serve and nurture everyone who seeks what you have to offer. The Earth Element helps you to treat every potential client as you would treat your clients, ready and willing to support them to get what they want.

The Metal Element helps you acknowledge your potential clients. Just as we revere trace minerals for the life they provide and gemstones that are of great value, the Metal Element is about seeing and acknowledging the brilliant diamond within everyone you meet. When you use the Metal Element in Heartselling™ conversations, you notice the potential client shining brightly and you let them know you see their magnificence.

The Water Element is the Element of curiosity. Imagine the ocean, pretty at the surface, but mysterious and profound as you discover its depths. This is the power of the Water Element. When you use curiosity in Heartselling™ conversations, you listen attentively to your potential client's needs and desires. You discover more about them so you can find out how you can help.

The Wood Element enables you to be bold, just like a shoot bursting from its shell. When you are bold, you powerfully give people a choice. So, in this Element, you give them a choice to take the next step.

The 5 Elements are a complete system. Miss any of the 5 Elements in your Heartselling™ conversations and it's like putting a nail in a tire. Your conversations will go flat and your potential clients will probably not sign up for your services.

But when all 5 Elements are present, you will leave your potential clients better than you found them, and many will turn into clients.

The effectiveness of your Heartselling™ conversations is determined by the quality of the questions you ask your potential client. As we go through each Element in the following chapters, you'll see for yourself how each one is essential to your Heartselling™ conversations and you'll learn powerful questions related to each one.

Action Step 1: Listen to the audio track of the sample Heartselling™ conversation with Sharla and Jan and take notes about the powerful questions Sharla asks Jan.

NOTES:

5

How to Use the Fire Element to Create Instant Connection with Potential Clients

The Fire Element is about connection. The season associated with Fire is summertime. Imagine laughing around a campfire and having fun with your friends enjoying the feeling of connection. This is a great metaphor to describe the feeling of Fire.

In the 5 Element model, your heart is related to the Fire Element. When you're meeting new people, you can use your Fire Element to connect.

One of the themes in many of our programs is that connection matters more than anything. It matters more than anything you say or do. Because when your potential client can feel the connection of your heart, you build rapport and trust. No one wants to work with someone when they don't feel that connection. Connection also helps you get over feeling nervous when you're meeting new people.

A simple way to create instant connection with anyone you meet

Many Holistic Practitioners and Coaches have told us they feel nervous about selling their services. When we ask them why, we often find out it's because they are so busy trying to avoid being "sales-y." If this describes you, you're not alone.

Note from Sharla: I remember going to networking events in Santa Cruz and I was sure I was the youngest person there. So, there I am walking into this event as a life coach and an acupuncturist thinking, "I feel so uncomfortable at these things!"

Then one day it dawned on me that I was so busy worrying about how I was being perceived that I wasn't really connecting with anyone.

Once I realized that if I could find a way to connect instantly with people I meet, I would stop feeling anxious and instead start engaging with others on a heart level.

There's a tool to create instant connection with anyone you meet. Before we share the tool, we want to share a little about the theory from Chinese Medicine behind why this works so well.

Did you know there are special "meridians" or "channels" on the surface of your body and they have acupuncture points along their path? These meridians are much like a stream or a river on the surface of your body—and when you touch a point along the meridian you send a stream of energy through it.

Since meridians are connected to internal organs, this stream of energy can infuse internal organs with positive change. This is how acupuncture works.

And did you know there are two meridians in each of your hands that are connected to your heart? One of these meridians is directly connected to your heart and the other meridian is connected to your heart via your Heart Protector, otherwise known as your pericardium, or covering of the heart.

HEART MERIDIAN AND HEART PROTECTOR MERIDIAN

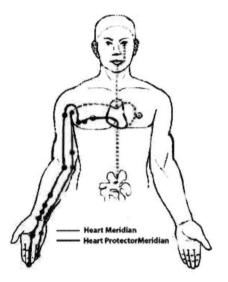

——— Heart Meridian
——— Heart ProtectorMeridian

Rub your hands together. When you pull them apart, can you feel the energy between them? This energy is moving between an acupuncture point on your Heart Protector Meridian (called "Laogong" or Heart Protector 8), which is in the center of your palm.

HEART PROTECTOR 8 (LAOGONG)

HP 8 Laogong

When you create this energy in your hands, you have the ability to create instant connection.

Note from Sharla: One way I got over feeling nervous at those networking events is by using the power of my Heart and Heart Protector Meridian in my hands.

Here's how you can do this in three easy steps:

1. Put your hands on you heart to really connect with your heart energy. Think about how you're going to meet some great people (like some of your clients you really love).

2. Take the energy from your heart and consciously put it in your hands (you can rub them together like the "Laogong" exercise above, if that helps).

3. When you shake the hand of someone you are meeting for the first time, take their hand between both of your hands so you are surrounding their hands with your heart energy you gathered earlier.

Just having that intention to send your heart energy to them, looking into their eyes, and being interested in them creates an instant connection.

Next time you're at an event where you're meeting new people, we encourage you to try this and notice how different it feels. This is especially helpful if you normally feel shy.

> **Action Step 2:** Practice using your heart energy when connecting with potential clients.

6

How to Use the Earth Element
to Serve Your Potential Clients

You just learned about the Fire Element. If you're not connected with your potential client, and they don't feel your warmth, they're not going to care what you have to say.

But without the Earth Element, your fiery enthusiasm could scare them away. The Earth Element grounds you in service, where instead of sharing all about your passion, you show up with a gift, with the intent to serve your potential client if it's a good match.

We shared earlier that "SELL" is actually a 5-letter word and should actually be spelled "S-E-R-V-E."

The reason so many Holistic Practitioners and Coaches have a tough time selling their services is that (1) they forget they are offering services and (2) the point is **to serve**. If you feel like a plastic salesperson one moment, while you are trying to convince a potential client to say yes, but a coach, practitioner or heart-based business owner in another moment, it can feel pretty awkward, because it's not authentic. So the good news is, in Heartselling™, **you get to be yourself.**

How can you do this? We believe that you should treat your potential clients as you would treat the people who are *already* your clients. When you're with your clients, you show up to serve them, and it should be the same with potential clients.

So your Heartselling™ conversations should be centered on serving the person in front of you.

How do you serve? **You find out if what they are looking for is something you can help them with** before you launch into your spiel about what you do.

When we meet someone new, we try to find out what is going on with them in their life and business so we can figure out how we can best serve them. Sometimes it means we recommend our own programs and sometimes it means we recommend someone else's products or services.

Wouldn't you rather share what you do with someone who has just said they need the exact thing you offer? This is what Heartselling™ is all about.

So in the Earth Element, you engage with potential clients from a state of service, and you ask questions to find out what they are looking for. This is what separates you from obnoxious, pushy salespeople.

Your job as a Heartseller™ is to care enough about what they want that you'll ask them what they want next in their life.

Yes, that's right. Ask them. While you may be very intuitive, the best way to find out what they want is to ask them. You don't have to guess. You just ask them. And we can almost guarantee that they'll love telling you. After all, how many people ask you *"What are you looking for next?"* and really listen to your answer?

The key to the Earth Element is: Attracting clients is not about you and your services. It is about your potential clients and what they want.

This is so important that we want you to say out loud, *"It's not about me, it's about them."*

Only when you know what they want can you provide it for them. When someone shares what they're looking for, you can serve them by offering your services if what they're looking for is what you offer. If what you offer isn't what they're looking for, you can serve them by referring them to someone who does provide what they're looking for.

Either way, you serve the person in front of you. When you serve others in this way, you will find that people will naturally refer others to you.

This is the power of being in the Earth Element. There is enough for everyone, and your goal is to help people get exactly what they want.

But let's face it, it can be challenging to be in this state of abundance when what you really need are new clients so that you can pay the bills.

Here's a secret to stepping into abundance. Dream out into the future when you are very successful and have more clients than you thought possible. Make that dream as vivid as you can, and whenever you start feeling desperate, just imagine that you've already arrived at that place where you have more than enough clients and you simply want clients for the sheer joy of contributing to them.

So, your job as a master Heartseller™ is to be what marketing guru Jay Abraham calls a "trusted advisor." As a trusted advisor, you care more about your potential client than you do about making a sale.

There is an expression, *"People have to know that you care before they care what you know."* As a trusted advisor, you show your care by listening first and speaking second.

Being a trusted advisor is a sacred responsibility. When someone is considering purchasing your services, they trust that you have their best interest in mind. Putting your own self-interest before your client's is one of the most damaging things you can do to your business long term.

As trusted advisors, it is one of our deepest honors when people call us or approach us at our workshops to ask us which program of ours we feel is best for them. We feel honored because our goal is to change the face of selling from selling to serving. When our potential clients trust us enough to ask our advice about what they should do next in their lives or businesses, it is very fulfilling to us.

We ask that you be a trusted advisor with your clients and keep their best interest in mind as you're having Heartselling™ conversations with them.

Here are some Earth questions to support you to serve as a trusted advisor. Earth questions are easy, open-ended, and designed to find out what your potential client wants.

Earth Questions/Statements:
"What are you up to and what are you looking for?"
"How can I support you in that?"
"If I could help you with that, is that something you'd be interested in hearing about?"
"What would most serve you right now?"

7

How to Use the Metal Element to Acknowledge Your Potential Clients

Now that you understand how to use the Fire and Earth Elements to connect with and serve your potential clients, you're ready to understand the missing ingredient in most sales conversations.

As a master Heartseller™, you know that when the conversation ends, you're either leaving people feeling better about themselves or worse about themselves. Without this Element, your clients will feel empty at the end of the conversation, as if there is something wrong with them.

And since we remember more about **how we felt** when we were with someone than about **what they said**, doesn't it make sense that you want to leave people feeling better than you found them? Wouldn't they be more likely to want to work with you in that case?

Would you like to know the secret to having people feel so good about themselves around you that they feel pulled to work with you? The secret is to acknowledge your potential clients often.

Why is acknowledgment part of the Metal Element?

In the 5 Element model, the Metal Element represents trace minerals, precious metals, and gemstones, which add quality to our water and soil and value to our lives.

If you think of the energy of autumn, which is the season associated with the Metal Element, it's the time when everything begins falling away and decomposing, and we often feel SAD—(diagnosed as "Seasonal Affect Disorder).

But in Chinese Medicine, it's perfectly normal to feel grief and sadness during this time of year. The leaves aren't the only things falling away! Without letting go of the things that no longer serve you, you would never be able to allow anything new into your life. And have you ever noticed that when you allow yourself to go through your grieving process (rather than trying to ignore it or push it away), the melancholy you feel is much like the energy of prayer? It's a way to get connected to the Divine.

The Metal Element represents the Heavenly Realms and helps you to recognize the Divine in each person you meet. It's like seeing the precious gem they are at their core that will never get scratched or marred in any way. It inspires you to see the shining diamond in everyone. When you acknowledge your potential clients, you are acknowledging the qualities of magnificence that you see in them.

Have you ever received an acknowledgment from someone that you remembered years later? Maybe you felt so seen and heard that it touched your soul and changed the way you felt about yourself.

When people learn about acknowledgment, they ask us, *"What is the difference between complimenting a potential client and acknowledging them?"*

Most people you meet are aching to be "seen" for who they really are. And they want to be seen in a deeper way than just a compliment. So, compliments are more superficial. They're about what someone does, like *"you did a great job!"* Or about what someone is wearing, like *"nice shirt."* Acknowledgments are about who they are BEING or some wonderful quality you see in them.

So how does this work in Heartselling™?

Depending on how connected you are, you may want to start with a compliment. A compliment opens the space for a deeper connection. And then, once you're feeling a deep connection, you can acknowledge your potential client.

How do you acknowledge your potential client?

When we have Heartselling™ conversations with potential clients, we allow ourselves to see the Divinity in them. We allow ourselves to see their brilliance and magnificence.

This is the key here: You want to look for something brilliant and magnificent about them. You can acknowledge them for many things including how they've grown, what you see that's wonderful about them right now, or what you see is possible for them to achieve.

Often when you acknowledge someone for what they can achieve, you're letting them know you believe in them.

When we have a Heartselling™ conversation, our potential client shares with us about their life and business and what they are most looking for (Earth Element). We feel their Heart and their intention to really make a difference, and we see their potential to fulfill on their dream. And, we can see them making hundreds of thousands of dollars.

As a Heartseller™, it's our job to see their amazing potential and what gifts they have to offer through their work. It's a huge acknowledgment to them, especially when so many others don't take the time to REALLY see their potential!

So, when you are in a Heartselling™ conversation, the Earth Element supports you to help them discover what they are looking for, and the Metal Element inspires you to encourage them to *feel* how great it will be when they get it.

Are they looking for pain relief, joy, success, love? Whatever they're looking for, it's important that you acknowledge them. You can acknowledge them for their courage for dealing with pain for this long or their willingness to step into the adventure of going after their big Vision.

When you acknowledge your potential client in this way, they often feel like there is no one else in the room but the two of you—and you will have people signing up right and left for your services.

We believe that the day when all people know how magnificent they are, that will be the day that war will cease. Kids will grow up with hearts filled with joy, for they will have nothing to prove. They will sink into their divinity, and from that space of heartfullness, create miracles.

Mastering the art of acknowledgment helps you to become a client magnet. As a master Heartseller™, your job is to deeply appreciate your potential client. In order for this to be effective, your acknowledgments must be authentic.

You have to believe that your potential client is awesome. Why? Because when you are in this state of appreciation, your potential client will feel it. And they will want more of it. Because most people don't receive the amount of appreciation they deserve.

What if you're not in the best mood? How do you authentically appreciate a potential client so you can acknowledge them? As a master Heartseller™, you ask your potential clients powerful questions. And as a master acknowledger, you ask yourself one powerful question: *"What is SO AMAZING about this person before me?"*

And if you focus on this question long enough, your bad mood will shift and you will find yourself naturally acknowledging this person, because that's what will be on your mind and in your heart.

And when people feel so seen by you they will naturally open to you, trust you, and be drawn to working with you. They will say to themselves: *"If I feel this good now, imagine how I'll feel when I am actually working with them."*

We highly recommend you continue the acknowledgment after they become your clients. Keep seeing the gem in them every time you meet them.

Your job is to help them solve their problems. But for every piece of negative feedback you give them, give them at least one piece of positive feedback. For example, if you are a massage therapist and you say, *"John, your shoulders feel very tense,"* make sure that you tell them what is great about their body also. Like, *"Your lower back is feeling really strong and limber"* or *"but your Spirit is shining really bright today."*

Questions to ask yourself to get into a state of appreciation for your potential client:
"What is so amazing about this Human Being?"
"What do I appreciate about this Human Being?"
"What do I love about this person?"
"What is great about them that they might not even get yet?"

Metal Element Acknowledgment Statements/Questions:
"What I appreciate about you is..."
"What I see in you is..."
"I get that you are committed to _____."

> **Action Step 3:** Use these acknowledging questions and statements in all your conversations and notice the impact it has on your potential clients.

As you become more comfortable with acknowledgment, you might notice that some people have a difficult time accepting compliments and acknowledgments. If this is the case, you can notice when their energy contracts. It may feel like they're leaning away.

And if you feel their energy contract, one thing you can do is to get curious with them about what has them shrink back from the acknowledgment.

We'll share about curiosity in the Water Element, but for now our challenge to you is to go out and acknowledge 3 people per day for the next week. The worst thing that could happen is you leave people in a better place than you found them. And you might even get some clients out of it.

How do you use the Metal Element to increase your Yes factor?

Just as the Metal Element is about minerals, metals, and gemstones, it is also connected to the archetypal "Father" energy. One crucial aspect of this archetype is offering respect.

When you respect another human being, you respect their time and their wishes. The key to being respectful is to ask permission. This skill will create a huge breakthrough in your ability to be an effective Heartseller™, so people will love to hear from you.

One of the reasons why salespeople have a bad name is because most salespeople don't ask permission. They don't ask if it's the best time, especially telemarketers.

So, whenever you call someone to initiate a Heartselling™ conversation, make sure that you tell them why you're calling and ask them if it's a good time.

And whenever you enter bold territory, ask permission to go further.

Especially when you first start using Heartselling™, you might feel a little apprehensive and awkward. That's totally normal. The best way to get over that awkwardness is to use the Metal Element to ask permission of your potential clients to go further.

Here are four great permission-based questions that you can practice using with your potential clients right away.

Metal Element Questions for asking permission:
"Is this a good time?"
"How does that sound?"
"Are you interested in hearing more?"
"Can I ask you a question about that?"

When you use the Metal Element in your Heartselling™ conversations, you will leave your potential clients feeling better than you found them and more interested in working with you further.

NOTES:

8

How to Use the Water Element to Be Curious With Your Potential Clients

Now that you've learned how to acknowledge your potential clients and leave them feeling better than how you found them, and you've seen the importance of respecting people and their time by asking permission, you're ready to dive into the Water Element.

The Water Element is the secret behind enjoying every Heartselling™ conversation you have. When you bring the Water Element of curiosity to each conversation, every potential client will be fresh, fascinating, and intriguing.

Instead of trying to convince your potential clients to try your services, when you are in the Water Element you'll find them talking themselves into working with you.

Most salespeople enter the conversation with a strong agenda to push their product or service. This type of sales conversation is all about closing the sale, and it ignores the most important person in the conversation: the potential client.

But Heartselling™ is changing all that!

How?

All you're doing is asking questions, and if your services are a match for your potential client, they'll discover that for themselves.

Isn't it refreshing when someone is curious about you? I love it when someone asks me to talk about myself, don't you?

When you give someone the opportunity to talk about themselves by being curious about them, it opens your potential clients up. Because most people are craving a good listener. And your listening itself can be very healing for them.

How does curiosity relate to the Water Element?

Think about the surface of the ocean. Sometimes it is really beautiful and sometimes it is choppy. But how often do you think about what's under the surface? If you go below the surface and into the depths, there is so much to discover.

Your potential clients are the same way. While you may think that they're just like everyone else, your potential client has an ocean of depth beneath the surface. You just have to go scuba diving to find it.

When you take the time to get curious about your potential clients, it shows you are interested and they will feel like someone cares about them. When you express genuine curiosity, it creates trust. And people are more likely to sign up for your services when they know, like, and trust you.

Before we share about the three types of curiosity and which type you'll want to use to support your potential clients in talking themselves into working with you, we've got to first discuss why most people aren't very curious.

Have you hung around a 5- or 6-year-old lately? Aren't they the most curious beings? Well, at some point a well-intentioned and often loving parent or friend or teacher just gets fed up with all the questions and they say something like: *"Stop asking so many questions,"* or if they're really fed up, *"Sit down and shut UP!"* This is where expressions like *"Curiosity killed the cat,"* and *"Children are to be seen but not heard,"* and *"Stop being so nosey"* come from.

So kids slowly learn to stifle their natural curiosity, and if you're like most people, this happened to you at some point. You stopped asking so many questions, but your curiosity is still there.

Did you know that 75% of your body is made up of water? Well, your curiosity did not evaporate just because you were told not to ask so many questions.

We've found that the more curious and interested you are in your potential clients, the more they'll share with you and the closer they'll get to saying Yes to your services.

It's time to reclaim your curiosity, so you can use this essential Element to be a client magnet.

Three Types of Curiosity

Type 1: Unadulterated Curiosity

Unadulterated curiosity is the curiosity of a child, before getting conditioned by adults not to be curious.

Anything goes. For example, questions like *"Why are you wearing your hair like that?"* and *"Why is the sky blue?"* are questions of unadulterated curiosity. It's about being totally fascinated with whatever and whoever is in front of you and asking any question that pops into your mind.

Type 2: Agenda Curiosity

Agenda curiosity is for your own sake or your own agenda. This type of curiosity is what most people refer to as being nosey. In other words, this is the type of curiosity you want to avoid.

Agenda curiosity is the type you might feel from a salesperson who is clearly interested in getting you to sign up for their product or service, whether or not it's in your own interest.

Type 3: Intentional Curiosity

Intentional curiosity does two things simultaneously. First, it helps your potential clients discover more about themselves. And second, it reveals whether or not they are perfect for your services.

This is when you get curious with your potential client about the problem you can help them with.

Unadulterated curiosity is great at the beginning of a conversation.

You can use questions such as:
"How are you?"
"Oh, tell me more about that."
"Very interesting, what's that like for you?"

But if you stay in unadulterated curiosity forever, you'll never get any clients.

So, after working with unadulterated curiosity, you will soon move into intentional curiosity.

There's a fine line between agenda curiosity, which can be damaging, and intentional curiosity, which can be healing.

When you're in the energy of agenda curiosity, you're thinking, *"I want this person to be my client no matter what."*

When you're in the energy of intentional curiosity, you're thinking, *"I want this person to be my client, if it's for the Highest Good of All Beings."*

Now, ultimately, you can't know what the Highest Good is, so it allows you to go on a journey of discovery with your potential client.

Here's an example of how to use intentional curiosity: If you are a chiropractor who specializes in helping people with migraine headaches, you might say something like this: *"Wow, after hearing all about your job, it sounds really stressful. Do you ever get headaches from all that stress?"* If they don't have the problem you can help them with, that's okay. This is a great time to let them know what you do and ask if they have any friends or colleagues that do get headaches.

However, if they do get headaches, ask them to tell you more about that. Keep exploring with them. You can ask questions like: *"What is that like for you?"* or *"Tell me more about that."*

Or let's say you're a coach who helps people transition from working a corporate job to a home-based business. And you're having a Heartselling™ conversation with a woman who is scared, frustrated, and probably feels she can't leave her job because of the money or benefits. Perhaps she really wants to start a business based out of her home. In this case, we recommend using curiosity to find out WHY she really wants to own a home-based business. Is it because she can be home with her kids? Is it because she wants more freedom?

You could get curious about what that home-based business will provide for her. At the same time that she is sharing with you why she wants this change, she is also revealing how she is your perfect client. The more curious you get, the deeper the conversation goes and the more she talks herself into working with you.

This is the power of the Water Element. When you are curious with a potential client, you experience them on a deep level. At the same time, they understand more about themselves. And together, you discover what they are looking for next.

The deeper you go, the more they'll trust you. The more they trust you, the more open they will be to sharing what they're most committed to. Once they share what they're looking for next, you can step into the Earth Element and how you can serve them and help them get what they most want. Or you can acknowledge them for their deep commitment and their courage. Or you can get even more curious, and ask them more about it, like *"How would it feel when you get what you are looking for?"*

Are you starting to see how the Elements work together?

Before you leave the Water Element of curiosity to move into the Wood Element, which is to boldly give them a choice, there is one last question you must ask. This is SO important! Whether you are offering them a $20,000 program or a free session, you must ask this question.

The question is:
"If we were to work together, what would you see yourself getting out of it?"

You can also ask it like this:
"What would you see yourself getting from working with me?"

Let them tell you what they see. Then you can say, *"Yes, exactly, you'll get a, b, and c, plus x, y, and z."*

Or, *"You know, I can't promise you that, but what I can promise you is x, y, and z."*

There are two reasons to ask this. First, as their trusted advisor, it is your job to make sure you can offer what they want to get from working with you. And second, to give them a space to get really excited about what they could get from working with you and to paint the picture in their own words. When you ask them that question, this is where they actually talk themselves into working with you. And you want them to be really excited before you ask them to take the next step, which might be to sign up for your services.

Ultimately, the deeper they go with you, the more likely it is that they'll become your client.

Water Element Questions:
"How's your _____(neck, job, life, dreams, or whatever you help people with)?"
"I'm curious, would you tell me more about that?"
"What else?"
"What's that like for you?"
"How is that affecting (your life, your business, your relationships)?"
"What do you want instead?"
"How would it feel if you got that?"
"If we were to work together, what would you see yourself getting out of it?"

Action Step 4:   Find someone to do this exercise with you. Be completely curious with them for 15 minutes. For the first 5 minutes, try on unadulterated curiosity with your buddy. You can ask them whatever you want to ask them.

Let them know before you start that they don't have to answer anything they don't want to.

Even if you know this person very well, your job is to see them, as if for the first time. Your job is to discover three new things about this person in five minutes. And support them to talk about the problem you can help with. If they have the problem, get even more curious with them.

Continue the conversation being curious about this person for 15 minutes non-stop. If you can be truly interested in them, you are on your way to using the Water Element masterfully.

This exercise will help you discover your natural curiosity so you can start using it to help potential clients talk themselves into working with you.

Deep Listening with the Water Element

Another important aspect of the Water Element is deep listening. In the Chinese model of the Five Elements, the ears are related to the Water Element. So deep listening is part of the Water Element and supports you in having amazing Heartselling™ conversations.

One powerful way to listen deeply is to listen like the person is already your client.

If you are a massage therapist who leaves people relaxed and rejuvenated, listen to them in a way that leaves them feeling relaxed and rejuvenated just from your conversation.

If you are a coach who empowers people, empower them while you are talking with them about being your client. The transition will feel much more natural for you. And you will be congruent, the same person having the Heartselling™ conversation with them as the one working with them as your client.

> **Action Step 5:** Have three conversations today, listening to your potential clients as if they already are your clients. Allow yourself to give them a taste of what it would be like to work with you before they even say Yes.

When you use the Water Element to get curious with your potential clients and listen to them deeply as if they are already your client, you open them up to their higher commitments. You support them to discover more about themselves while they talk themselves into working with you.

NOTES:

9

How to Use the Wood Element to Give Your Potential Clients a Choice

Now that you've learned how to connect, serve, acknowledge, and be curious...now what? It's time to use the Wood Element, which is the most com n Element mo that most practitioners and coaches are missing.

We've found that most Holistic Practitioners and Coaches are uncomfortable with asking potential clients to boldly make a choice during a Heartselling™ conversation. Instead, they shyly hand out their business card and hope the potential client calls them for a session.

That hope usually does not come to fruition, because every day people are bombarded with thousands of marketing messages. After a couple of days, your potential client is probably not thinking about you any longer.

Consider this for a moment. How many people have handed you business cards over the last year? And how many of those people did *you* call about their services? You probably didn't call many of them. And so it is when you hand people your business card and hope they call. Instead, you must give them a choice, even though it may feel uncomfortable at first.

There is a saying, *"Your success is equal to the number of uncomfortable conversations you're willing to have."* And it's only uncomfortable in the beginning while you're learning.
Eventually, it gets easier, just like everything else you've learned in life, and it will become second nature.

The Wood Element is about giving people a choice.

If you practice what we're going to share with you in this chapter alone, you can double your income very quickly.

How is the Wood Element about giving someone a choice?

Think about a seedling or an acorn in the springtime. Housed inside of it is the plan to grow into an oak tree. It has to burst from its shell and then grow around all the rocks and roots and then finally it breaks the surface of the ground. Then there are huge trees surrounding it...but it has a Vision to become an oak tree. It's going to grow toward the light no matter what. This no-matter-what "decision" is what enables it to thrive.

This is the power of the Wood Element. It's the boldness and decisiveness needed to take a stand for other people's lives and give them a choice.

Because when you don't ask, the answer is always No. When you do ask, you give people the opportunity to say Yes to what their heart is calling them to say Yes to.

But many practitioners and coaches feel so afraid of hearing the word No that they don't ask.

Handing someone your business card and saying *"Call me if you would like a session"* is not giving them a choice. Asking *"Can we follow up on Tuesday about our conversation today?" "Would you like to get started?"* or *"Would you like to schedule a session?"* is giving people a choice. Your potential client gets to say Yes or No.

It takes courage to be in the Wood Element in Heartselling™ conversations. Are you willing to be courageous for the sake of your clients getting what they want most in their lives? If so, you will embrace the Wood Element.

Just to clarify, there are a lot of sales trainings that teach "assumptive selling." An example of this is asking: *"Would you like to come in next Tuesday or Thursday?"* before they even said they want to come in for a session with you.

This is disrespectful, because it doesn't allow your potential client to fully choose working with you. It feels pushy and is a hard-selling technique.

You want your clients to be fully aligned with their Yes or fully aligned with their No. Because when they're aligned at the beginning and fully choose your services at the beginning, they are more likely to be aligned throughout your time of working together.

You only want people to be your clients who really want to be your clients. Do not convince or cajole them. Instead, give them a clear choice and delight in their Yes or No.

Now, giving them a choice doesn't always mean a choice to sign up right now. Until you've connected with them, served them, acknowledged them, and been curious with them, they are probably not ready to be your client.

Heartselling™ conversations take time, and if you only have 5 or 10 minutes, it's usually not enough time to ask them to be your client. In that case, giving them a choice can be inviting them to talk with you at a future time and date.

We were at an event where we discovered during a conversation that a woman named Sheri had a coaching practice for 2 years, but wasn't really earning a living as a coach. She wanted to quit her job and have enough clients to enjoy her life and stop working a job she didn't enjoy.

She knew coaching was her "Divine Right Livelihood" and was ready to take the next steps.

We felt it was appropriate for her to participate in our Double Your Practice in 90 Days Program, so she could finally get the structure and support to reach her goal. But we were at a seminar, the break was over, and it was time to go back to our seats.

She still had questions about the program, and it wouldn't have made sense to give her a choice to sign up for the program or not at that time.

So instead of trying to "close the sale," we said: *"It sounds like you're looking to get the support to quit your day job and be a full-time coach. If we had a program that could support you to easily make that transition, would you be interested in hearing about it?"*

She said, *"Absolutely!"*

"Well, since we need to get back to our seats, we'd love to follow up with you by phone. Do you have a business card?"

She handed us her business card and we said, *"Would Tuesday of next week be a good time to connect about this so we can hear more about your coaching practice and see if what we have to offer is a good match for what you are looking for?"*

She said, *"Please call me on Tuesday. I'm looking forward to it."*

We took it one step further, *"What time would work best for you on Tuesday?"*

We contacted her on Tuesday and after a couple of Heartselling™ conversations, she signed up for the program.

Unless you get a specific time, you could play phone tag for weeks. Or you might call on Tuesday as she's on her way out the door. So, you try again on Thursday, and by the time you reach each other, two weeks have gone by and she barely remembers the conversation she had with you.

When you are first getting to know someone, it isn't wise to try to "close the sale." The key is you need to make sure that they're leaning in and excited before you step into Wood and boldly give them a choice.

Only after they have opened up toward their highest commitment should you use the Wood Element to give them a choice to sign up for your services.

As we said earlier, many Holistic Practitioners and Coaches are afraid to hear the word No, and so they don't give their potential clients a clear choice. If you do give them a choice to either follow up or sign up for your services, you've just increased your chances of getting new clients, and if you never ask, you're leaving thousands of dollars on the table.

This is how using the Wood Element can double your income in a very short period of time.

Wood Element Questions to help you give them a choice:
"Would you like to sign up for the program?"
"Would you like to schedule a session?"
"Would you like to get started?"
"Can I follow up with you in a few days?"

Now here's the secret. When you ask and they say "No," we want you to think of these two things. First, every No you get is moving you closer to getting a Yes. Second, when they say No, you have been spared. You don't have to know why, but for whatever reason, it was not in divine order for you to be working with this person at this time. When you think of it like *"I was just spared,"* it will give you the permission to allow yourself to get as many No's as you need to get your Yes's.

Most people are afraid to hear the word No. The best recipe to break through this fear is to go out and collect No's.

Action Step 6: Get 20 No's this week. Yes, that's exactly right. Go out and get 20 No's. By getting a lot of No's out of the way, it will free you to get lots of Yes's. And, who knows, one of your No's might actually say Yes.

Either way, you win. If they say No, you win because you were collecting No's, and if they say Yes, you win because you'll get a new client. This exercise may be your most important homework that you take on. Many of our clients have felt completely liberated from fear of rejection after doing this exercise.

The Wood Element helps you to give them a choice. With practice, it will become easy and graceful to use the Wood Element in your Heartselling™ conversations.

10

How the 6 Stages of Heartselling™ Give You the Confidence of a Heartselling™ Master

1. Open the conversation
2. Find out what they're looking for
3. Share a resource
4. See if you're a match
5. Ask them to take the next step
6. Dance with concerns

When we first started teaching Heartselling™, we didn't have the 6 Stages of a Heartselling™ conversation. We taught only the 5 Elements, and our clients doubled their practices and got tremendous results.

But when some of our clients started asking us if there was a more linear model to Heartselling™, we had to say *"No, because Heartselling™ is a dance between the Elements, and every Heartselling™ conversation is totally different from the next."*

Note from Jesse: Last year, I was listening to Sharla having a Heartselling™ conversation at a Rejuvenate Your Practice 2 Day Intensive, and I noticed that she was going through the same 6 Stages that she always did in every Heartselling™ conversation. I realized that I was doing the same thing. I was ecstatic. We finally had a linear, step-by-step model to teach others the overall flow of a conversation.

Because it's linear, this model of the 6 Stages gives you the tools to systematically create great Heartselling™ results and always know where you are in a Heartselling™ conversation.

After opening your conversation, you find out what they're looking for. Then you share a resource that could help them. Then you see if that resource is a good match. Then you ask them to take the next step, either a follow-up conversation or to get started working with you. Then, you dance with concerns if they come up.

Because Heartselling™ conversations often take time you may need to have 2 or 3 conversations with a potential client to complete all 6 Stages.

Your potential clients may say things that force you to skip stages. With practice, you'll learn to gracefully navigate your way around the stages. When you learn the 6 Stages, you'll always know where you are in a Heartselling™ conversation, which will give you the confidence you need to become a Heartselling™ master.

11

Stage 1:
How to Gracefully Open a Conversation
with a Potential Client

1. Open the conversation

A lot of people don't have Heartselling™ conversations because they feel awkward opening the conversation. We've got bad news, good news, and even better news. The bad news is that your level of success in Heartselling™ will be equal to the number of potentially uncomfortable conversations you're willing to start. The good news is that if it is awkward for you to start, it will become less and less awkward, the more conversations you have.

The even better news is this: How you open a Heartselling™ conversation is how you would open any conversation. You don't have to get them to be your client right away. Your sole intention for Stage 1 is to connect with another human being. The key is to be totally natural.

The problem is that even though human beings are very social animals, we spend so much time in front of electronic boxes like computers, TVs, and iphones. For this and many other reasons, a lot of people are out of practice when it comes to opening conversations, especially with people they don't know or don't know well.

Before you get concerned that you'll have to make a lot of cold calls, don't worry. A master Heartseller™ doesn't make cold calls from a phone book. Instead, you're going to start with people you know--your friends and clients--and ask them for referrals.

But after a while, you may run out of friends and clients who might refer you to others, and you may have to **meet some new people.**

Now, your mother may have told you not to talk with strangers, but we're here to tell you that it's okay to talk with strangers. In fact, at some point everyone in your life was a "stranger."

While it might feel uncomfortable at first, you get to practice stepping out of your comfort zone. And soon the expansion of your comfort zone will actually bring you a feeling of confidence, ease, and freedom.

To make this easier for you, you can let the 5 Elements of Heartselling™ support you to create new connections with people who will be grateful for the gift of your attention to them.

So, in Stage 1, you choose an Element before you start the conversation.

Using the Fire Element to Open the Conversation

Fire is about connection. We shared earlier that by getting present to your heart energy and allowing it to flow through your hands, you can shake hands with someone and transmit your heart energy to them. This is a great way to connect your heart with their heart.

The Fire Element is also about play and laughter and fun. So, if you can have one good laugh, it can erase any awkwardness.

You can also find something you have in common, to build rapport. This alone can create enough connection for you to move into Stage 2.

Using the Earth Element to Open the Conversation

The Earth Element is all about service. When you're in the Earth Element, you find opportunities to serve others as a way to open the conversation.

Perhaps you're watching your son or daughter play soccer, and you overhear one of the other moms saying that she needs to make a phone call but she forgot her phone. If you have a cell phone, you could offer to let her borrow yours.

If you're walking into a store, you might open a door for the person behind you, which might be the beginning of a conversation.

If you're an energy worker or bodyworker and you overhear someone complaining of a neck ache, you might offer to do 5 minutes of work on them if it feels appropriate.

If you're a coach and someone is complaining about something, you may offer to make a suggestion or give them feedback.

Your mantra is, *"How can I help?"* You can even ask the Universe to put you in situations all day long where you can open your conversations by serving people.

We've found that your intention shows up before you do. When people feel your intention to serve, they will be drawn to you and the conversation will begin quite naturally.

Using the Metal Element to Open the Conversation

The Metal Element is about acknowledging the diamond in the person you're speaking with. This is one of our favorite ways to start a conversation, because no matter if the conversation progresses into a full-fledged Heartselling™ conversation or not, we know that we're both guaranteed to leave the conversation feeling better than we started.

> **Action Step 7:** Compliment ten people a day for a week. And if the compliments go well, you can move into an acknowledgment as you get to know them better.

Using the Water Element to Open the Conversation

The Water Element is about Curiosity. This is a fun way to start Heartselling™ conversations. You can open the conversation by saying, *"I'm curious..."* and see what pops out of your mouth next.

For example, let's say you're in a bookstore and you notice someone reading a book. You could say, *"I'm curious, I was looking for that book. What do you think about (the topic)?"*

This isn't a gimmick or technique, but a way to authentically open the conversation if you really were interested in the book they have in their hands.

Another example is if you're at a networking event, standing at the buffet, you could simply say, *"I'm curious, how is that salsa? Is it really hot?"*

Or, if you're at a party, you can say, *"I'm curious, how long have you known the host?"*

When you use the Water Element to open the conversation, you never know what you'll discover.

Using the Wood Element to Open the Conversation

Wood is the Element where you give them a choice. It's direct, focused, and strong. It's a great way to end conversations, but if you start conversations with the Wood Element, you might come across as pushy.

However, you may just insert yourself into a conversation at a networking event by saying something like, *"Hi there, I'm just going to insert myself here."*

Note from Sharla: I was at a high level networking event where I wanted to talk with a particular person and every time I looked over, he was in conversation with someone else. So, although it was a bit awkward, I walked up with confidence and just said, "Hi there, I'm just going to insert myself here." And I made the connection with this man.

If you're feeling shy or awkward about opening conversations, you may need to step into the energy of the Wood Element. It is the energy of an acorn that breaks out of its shell and shoots up and around rocks to the surface of the earth. Once there, it keeps growing toward the light. It may take this strength simply to approach people. But once you get there, we recommend you use the other 4 Elements to open the conversation and save the Wood Element of giving people a choice for later.

You just learned the 5 Elements to opening Heartselling™ conversations so that people love connecting with you. Most people find that one of these Elements will be much more comfortable than others to open conversations with.

We recommend you use your strongest Element. And then try out the other Elements. You might be surprised at how easy it is to relate to someone new when using the Elements.

How do you know when to move on to Stage 2? You'll know when you feel a warmth and comfort between you. A resonance, like you're vibrating at the same level, you're on the same page, or you're two chords resonating in harmony with each other. And here's the secret. The more connected you are, the more people trust you and the more permission you have to ask bold questions in Stages 2 to 6.

12

Stage 2: How to Serve Them and Find Out What They're Looking For

> **2. Find out what they're looking for**

So, now you've opened the conversation. You're feeling connected. But you don't know if they are a potential client yet, because you don't yet know what they're looking for.

As you discovered in the Earth Element, until you know what they're looking for, you have no idea whether you can serve them or not.

Imagine having a date over for dinner at your house. You want to prepare your best, most delicious meal.

You decide to cook an elaborate, gourmet, meat lasagna. Unfortunately, you didn't ask your date what they were "looking for," and your date is a vegetarian. As you put the meat lasagna in the refrigerator and head out the door to a restaurant, you vow to always ask a new date what type of food they like before planning a meal.

Similarly, if you don't find out what your potential clients are looking for, you could have the best services in the world and you could explain every last detail of how you can help them, but if they're not looking for what you've got, they're not going to be interested.

So, how do you find out what they're looking for? The most important question to ask to turn a social conversation into a

Heartselling™ conversation is, *"What are you up to and what are you looking for next?"*

When you ask this question, you're taking the lead and directing them into a Heartselling™ conversation.

Now if they ask you what you do before you ask them what they're up to and what they're looking for next, then they've moved the conversation to Stage 3 prematurely.

Don't worry. You can simply tell them what you do and then ask them about themselves.

Once they start telling you what they're looking for, you can use intentional curiosity to direct the conversation toward what you help people with.

For example, if you help people relieve back pain, you're going to start to move the conversation in the direction of their back.

Again, you don't have to rush this. It may take you a few minutes to get there. But you are looking for a segue into a conversation about the problem you solve.

One of the reasons it's so important to solve a problem for people is that it becomes very obvious when people are your potential clients and when they're not.

If they don't have the problem you solve, then they're not your potential client.

But if you can offer them a great resource that helps them get what they are looking for, they will often be so grateful that they may send you great referrals.

The key to mastering Stage 2 is to know the phrases that indicate that they've got the problem you solve.

For example, if we hear that someone is a coach, holistic practitioner, or heart-based business owner, they may be a potential client of ours.

We know we can support them if they say some variation on the following: *"I wish I was making more money. I really love serving and I don't have as many clients as I want."*

If you help relieve back pain, a key phrase to listen for would be: *"My back is killing me."*

If you work with couples who want more romance, listen for something like: *"I know we love each other, but we've lost that spark."*

> **Action Step 8:** Brainstorm 5 phrases that indicate a potential client has the problem you can solve.

The great thing about knowing the phrases that indicate someone would be a great client for you is that you're sending out an order to the Universe to send people with that problem to you. But not everyone will have the problem you solve.

If you get intentionally curious with them about the problem you solve and it turns out that they don't have that problem, great!

You have a choice. You can either gracefully end the Heartselling™ conversation, or, knowing that whatever you give returns to you, you can recommend a resource that would support them with what they are looking for.

But if your potential client does say a phrase that indicates that you can help, you've just struck gold. But before you tell them that you've got the solution to their problem, you've got to dig a little deeper so that they are really hungry for your solution.

When they share a variation of one of the phrases that you just brainstormed, here are some questions you can ask:

Question 1: *"How is that for you?"*
"Wow, that sounds _____(challenging, terrible, frustrating, etc.) Say some more about that."

Question 2: *"What do you want instead?"*

This puts them on the track of possibility and excitement...and they'll get present to the solution they want.

Question 3: *"How would your life change if you had that?"*

Once they've answered these questions, their problem will be more in the forefront of their mind, and you will increase their desire for the solution to that problem. They will be primed for Stage 3, which is where you get to share the resource (which in many cases happens to be your service) that would most support them to get what they said they wanted.

13

Stage 3:
Share an Appropriate Resource with Your Potential Client

3. Share a resource

In Stage 2 your potential clients became aware of a problem and got clear about what they wanted instead. And now they are thinking about how great it will be when they get that solution.

This is an excellent time to share about what you do, because it will be offering them a solution to their problem. This is where you share a resource in a natural and authentic way. You'll make a recommendation to support them to get what they're looking for.

Now, instead of tuning out when you share what you do, they will be very grateful to hear it, because it will be about helping them get the solution they're craving. Instead of seeing what you do as an attempt to get them to buy something, they'll see your services as a gift.

They might think, *"Oh my gosh, I was waiting for you."*

You are now in Stage 3, which is to share a resource, whether it's your own services or someone else's.

But, hang on a second...

Just before you share a resource, you want to transition into

Stage 3 by asking the question: *"If I could help you with that (the solution they're looking for), is that something you would like to hear more about?"*

We ask this question in every Heartselling™ conversation we have.

If you've set up Stage 1 and Stage 2 well, it will be so natural for you to ask this question. And when they say, *"YES, PLEASE!"* then you know they're interested in hearing more.

Now, it's your time to share your "What do you do?" statement.

Action Step 9: Craft your "What do you do?" statement.

We've got a simple template for sharing about what you do.

"You know how some (people/women/your niche market) have _____ (the problem you solve)?   Well, I (help/teach/support) them to _____ (solution you provide)."

You can fill in the blanks so you can share your services as a powerful resource for your potential clients.

Here's an example of how this part of the conversation might go:
Let's say we're having a conversation with a Holistic Practitioner or Coach. They've told us they want more clients.

So we say, *"How is that for you, not having as many clients as you want?"*

They share more about the problem. Then we really acknowledge how challenging or frustrating that must be for them.

So we ask, *"How do you want it to be instead?"* And they tell us about what they want instead.

And then we ask, *"How would that be if you got that?"* And they get excited about it.

And then we say, *"If we could help you with that, is that something you'd be interested in hearing more about that?"*

They say, *"Absolutely."*

"You know, that's exactly what we do, we teach people how to get more clients (or whatever you offer)."

This is when you share your "What do you do?" statement.

And it will come out so naturally. Stage 3 occurs as an authentic and generous recommendation, and they will be so grateful that you shared it.

NOTES:

_____
_____
_____
_____
_____
_____
_____
_____
_____
_____
_____
_____
_____
_____
_____
_____
_____
_____
_____
_____
_____
_____
_____
_____
_____
_____
_____
_____
_____
_____
_____

14

Stage 4:
See If You're a Match as Your Potential Client Talks Themselves Into Working with You

4. See if you're a match

In Stage 3, you shared a resource. It was either someone else's services (if they didn't have the problem you solve) or your own services (also known as your "What do you do?" statement.)

They're engaged and excited because they see that what you're offering may really be able to support them. You're now ready for Stage 4, which is to see if you're a match.

Now most people get so excited about being able to support their potential clients that they start going on and on about how they can help.

That is the worst thing you can do at this point.

The more you talk, the less interested they will become. There is an expression: *"There are those who have talked themselves out of a sale, but no one has ever listened themselves out of a sale."*

KEY POINT: Instead of trying to talk them into your services, you allow them to talk themselves into your services by asking them a sequence of questions after sharing about your services.

The following questions will help your potential clients talk themselves into working with you:

- *"How does that sound to you?"*

- *"What would you see yourself getting out of working with me?"* (You want to find out what results they are seeking.)

- When they share what they see themselves getting out of working with you, ask them: *"Do you have any questions?"*

- Once you answer their questions briefly and with benefit-laden language, you ask them, *"Imagine you were able to _____ (get the result they want), how would that benefit your whole life?"*

- *"What would it be worth to you?"*

- *"What's the next step?"*

Now, keep in mind that people are not robots, and your conversation may not go exactly in this order. These questions simply serve as a guide, not a fixed formula.

And since you also have the 5 Elements, you'll dance through the Elements as you ask these questions. For example, halfway through the conversation, you may acknowledge them or ask them a curious question that helps them go deeper, like *"Would you say some more about that?"*

After you share what you do, they may immediately ask how much you charge. It's a reasonable question, and it's actually a "buying question." It means that they're interested in your services. But if you answer that question before they're really clear about the results they'll get from your services, your price tag could scare them off.

Here's a great thing to say if they ask you how much you charge before they're clear about the results they can get:

"You know, I'd love to share with you how much my services cost, but before I do, I'd love to hear a little bit more about what you'd want to get out of my services, so I can make sure it's a good fit for you."

You might offer different packages or programs. If you do, this is a really important response. Because you can't really answer the question, *"How much do you charge?"* until you find out more about what would be an appropriate fit for them.

Here's what we say:

"I'd love to answer that question, but before I do, I'd like to know a little bit more about what you're looking for and what results you're looking to get so I can make the best recommendation and then the price would be different based on whatever I recommend. So, can I hear a little bit more about you?"

We've found that the best time to share how much we charge is toward the end of the conversation, when you ask them if they have any questions. Since they've already told you what they want to get out of your services and you've helped them increase their desire and commitment level, they're now ready to have the money conversation.

In Stage 5, you ask them to take the next step. You'll know it's time to move into Stage 5 when either of you has to end the conversation for any reason or your potential client has all their questions answered and is very excited about getting started with you.

The next chapter will give you the most graceful ways to ask them to take the next step with you.

NOTES:

15

Stage 5:
How to Know When and How to
Ask Them To Take the Next Step

5. Ask them to take the next step

As a Heartseller™, you're like a yoga teacher. Your job is to stretch them a little bit further than they would go by themselves. And the best way to do that is to end every Heartselling™ conversation by asking them to take the next step.

Now, because Heartselling™ conversations take time, they often take more than one conversation. And the more clearly you have defined your niche, the shorter your Heartselling™ conversations will be.

Often, if you're at a party or networking event, you may not have the time to have a 30-minute Heartselling™ conversation with someone. You may have gotten interrupted in Stage 2, where you're finding out what they're looking for. Or maybe you were in Stage 3 and you shared what you do and they had to leave. Or maybe you were seeing if you were a match in Stage 4, but they still had questions.

No matter what stage you're in, if either of you has to end the conversation before it's time for you to ask them to get started in working with you, it's crucial that you jump into Stage 5 before you depart.

The next step may be a follow-up conversation. It may sound like this:

"It sounds like you're looking for X, Y, and Z result. I'd love to support you to get that. Would you like to continue this conversation so that I can help you get X, Y, and Z result?"

"Great. When would you like to talk?"

If it's possible, get their telephone number. It's much better if you set up an appointment in your calendars to talk. Otherwise, you could play phone tag for weeks until they hardly remember your conversation.

But if either of you don't have your calendars, your next best bet is to ask them, *"When would be the best time to call you?"*

So, if you've opened the conversation, found out what they're looking for, shared a resource, and seen that you are a match, you're now ready to ask them if they're ready to get started working with you.

It's like you're at the end of a fantastic first date. Your date is standing outside the door, jingling their keys, waiting for you to lean in for the kiss. You feel this person leaning in a little, waiting expectantly, excitedly for the kiss…

It's an exciting moment, and it only happens when you have the courage to hear a Yes or a No.

This is one of the key turning points in your Heartselling™ conversation, and we've seen so many or our clients who are new to Heartselling™ miss this important opportunity. The client is leaning in, they've basically told you they're really interested…and all you have to do is ASK.

You might find when you are starting out in Heartselling™ that you'll miss this key moment and then you'll evaluate your conversation and realize you missed it. But with practice, you'll know when it is the right time to ask them to take the next step, and it will become natural for you.

Until you get to the point where you absolutely recognize when this key moment occurs, you've got to start by being willing to ask.

Heartselling™ starts out as a numbers game. As you talk with more potential clients, your skills in Heartselling™ increase dramatically. And when you become a better Heartseller™, you get more clients. Boldly asking people to get started with you is the key to getting those clients.

Most Holistic Practitioners and Coaches shyly hand people a business card so as to not appear pushy and ask people to call them when they're interested.

We understand, because we've done it too.

But, if you don't ask the question, the answer is ALWAYS No. It takes courage to grow your business, and this moment in the Heartselling™ conversation is where the rubber meets the road.

There are 2 simple questions that will give you the keys to the practice of your dreams.

The first question is: *"Great, would you like to get started?"*

The second question is: *"When would you like to set up the first session?"*

Practice saying these phrases over and over in front of the mirror.

Once you've asked them to take the next step, you'll sometimes hear concerns about money or time or some other hesitation. That's why Stage 6 is about how to dance with concerns to turn half of your No's into Yes's.

16

Stage 6:
How to Dance with Concerns
to Double Your Practice

If they say Yes in Stage 5, then you don't have to move into Stage 6. But often you'll find that you'll ask people if they'd like to get started and they'll have concerns.

For most people, the 3 most common concerns are: *"I can't afford it," "I don't have the time,"* or *"I need to think about it."* And for most Holistic Practitioners and Coaches, this is the end of the conversation. But for a master Heartseller™, it marks the beginning of a new conversation, a potentially very healing conversation.

Once you start dancing with concerns, you're in Stage 6. And when you become masterful at dancing with concerns, you'll turn more than half of your No's into Yes's. This skill alone has the power to make or break your business. When we learned how to dance with concerns rather than give up at this stage of the conversation, our income literally doubled. And the same thing happened for so many of our clients.

The first key to dancing with concerns is to welcome their concern. Inwardly, you want to say *"YES!"* Because here's where you can really support them. And if you meet their concern with resistance, it will become a tug of war that you'll most likely lose.

It's important to realize that not everyone is supposed to be your client. With over six billion people on the planet, you don't need everyone to be your client. But we believe that, just as there are certain people who are divinely appointed to be in our programs, there are certain people who are divinely appointed to be your clients.

This is why this stage turns only half of your No's into Yes's.

Many sales trainings teach you how to deal with objections and give you scripted responses designed to manipulate people into saying Yes to something that's not going to serve them. It's called "closing the sale at all costs."

At Rejuvenate Training, we don't teach you how to "close the sale." We don't teach you scripts to manipulate people into saying Yes to something that is not going to serve them. We teach you how to open your potential clients to their own truth.

And when you help your potential clients discover their own truth, they will usually either become your client or send lots of people your way.

So, instead of giving you scripted responses to a concern that your potential client may have, we offer Magic Questions that open your potential clients to what they truly want, questions that help them get present to what they are most committed to. And in the presence of their deep commitment, their concerns dissolve.

But let us warn you that these questions work only when your intention is to serve.

Concern 1: "I can't afford it."

If someone says: *"I can't afford your services,"* it might or might not be true. Think about this: If your mother was in the hospital, and you needed to come up with $20,000 to save her life, would you come up with it? Would you find the time to support her? Would you need to think about it? Hopefully not too long.

And with the trillions of dollars that are being exchanged every day in our country, most people would have the wherewithal to come up with whatever you charge if they wanted it badly enough.

We had a woman who was in our Rejuvenate Your Practice 2 Day Intensive who really wanted to sign up for our 6 Figure Success Circle Program. She stomped her foot, and announced, *"I am a mother of 3, I home-school my kids, and I have 4 dollars in my pocket and that's it."*

As she was sharing this, we could feel a lot of people in our workshop sink into her story. But we would not. We told her that if she really wanted it, she would find the resources. In fact, we said, *"There is probably someone in the room who would fund the program for you."*

Later that day, an angel in the room anonymously paid for her first 3 months. She was so moved that she announced to the group that she was going to do one of our Rejuvenate U™ programs. Later that week, she walked into our office with a check for almost $12,000.

Since then, she has become one of our best, most committed clients, and because of her strong commitment and passion she

is changing the lives of many other mothers with her services.

When people really want something, they'll find a way to get it.

We've had many clients sign up for a package of programs that felt like a big time and money investment and weren't sure how they were going to pay for it. Many of them have manifested miracles because they were so committed to the results they saw were possible out of completing their work with us. And their results have been breathtaking, matching their commitment to success.

One of our clients had just moved to a new town. She was not sure how she would pay for the programs, especially since she didn't know anyone in this new town. But she had a strong commitment and using what she learned from us she started leading 2-hour workshops and filled her private practice in just a few months.

"I can't afford it" often really means: *"I haven't seen the value…yet."*

Instead of trying to convince people of the value, we're going to share 6 Magic Questions that will turn many of your No's into Yes's.

Remember that not everyone is your client. People will spend their money somewhere. And your job as their trusted advisor is to help them discover what they're most committed to and to help them invest their money in that direction.

When we first started our practices, so many times we were told that a potential client couldn't afford it, only to see them a couple of months later with a tan they got from a 7-day vacation in Hawaii or we would see them 3 months later and they would be working with a different coach.

If we had these 6 Magic Questions back then, it would have made a huge difference in our ability to get new clients.

Here are the 6 Magic Questions for dancing with the concern *"I can't afford it."*

Magic Question 1: *"May I ask you a question about that?"*

Start with this question because you are about to enter bold territory and you want to get permission to do so.

If you're like most people, you've used the words: *"I can't afford it,"* as an excuse for not buying something. Most people won't bother you once you say that, so if you're going to enter that territory, it's important to do so as respectfully as possible.

Magic Question 2: *"If it weren't for the money, is this something you would want to move forward with?"*

This question clarifies if they believe money is the real issue for them or if there's really something underneath the money concern.

If they say *"YES, absolutely!"* you've just found out that they BELIEVE money is really the obstacle.

At this point, you have 3 options:

Option 1: If you are very connected with them, you can say: *"It sounds like money is the only thing that's stopping you from getting (the result they want.)"* And you can continue to get curious with them using some of the Magic Questions below.

Option 2: You can offer a full scholarship, partial scholarship, or trade. But be cautious! If you often give yourself and your services away, we recommend not doing this, or doing it only for a pre-set number of people.

Option 3: You can refer them to another heart-based business owner who does what you do for a lesser price.

Magic Question 3: *"Can I ask you something? Assuming money wasn't an issue, what would you have to get out of it to make it worth it for you?"*

This question helps them put the money issue aside for a moment, so they can be open to finding a new way to make things work. So we ask:

Magic Question 4: *"Would you be open to brainstorming some possibilities of how you can come up with the money?"*

If they say Yes, ask them to start, and let them do as much of the brainstorming as possible. You can contribute ideas if it feels appropriate. (Possible resources are friends, family, relatives, loans, credit lines, credit cards, CDs, mutual funds, etc.).

We've found that when people want something, they do find a way. We can't tell you how many times our potential clients have really believed they weren't resourceful enough to find the money to pay for their education with us... and then found a way.

If you've done some brainstorming and they don't see a way, you can get curious and ask more questions or make special arrangements, take payments, whatever you and your client decide would be feasible.

If they say: *"No, I would not move forward with this,"* then we recommend honoring their "No" by thanking them. Without trying to convince them or get them to say *Yes,* you can get curious with them.

You can ask Magic Question 5: *"I'm curious, can you tell me a little bit more about why you're saying No? I'm not trying to get you to say Yes, I'm just curious."*

This will either open the Heartselling™ conversation back up into a space of possibility or it will just give you more information as to how to make your services more attractive.

If they say *"Yeah"* hesitantly, then it often means it really isn't the money.

It could be that they don't think they deserve the results they want, or they may not think that it will work for them or that they'll have the discipline to follow through, or 100 other possible things. But you will never get to what is underneath their money concern unless you ask Magic Question 6.

Here's Magic Question 6: *"You sound hesitant. Is there something else?"*

This opens up a space where you can get curious and find out what's going on for them, and they will probably share additional concerns at this time.

After you've uncovered these concerns and supported them to work with these concerns and have discovered it's something other than the money, you can simply ask Magic Question 3 again: *"What would you have to get out of my services to make it worthwhile for you?"*

At this point, you step into the role of trusted advisor.
You can tell them, *"Yes, absolutely you can get this"* or *"No, I can't promise you that, but here's what I can tell you."*

Often you will have to stand in a strong belief in your potential clients (and YOUR services) during this stage of the conversation. Sometimes you will need to have more faith in your potential clients than they have in themselves. One of the main reasons why someone might be hiring you is because they need to know that someone believes in them, even when they can't believe in themselves. So if you fail to show them that you believe in their ability to overcome whatever obstacle is in the way of them getting the result they want (money included), why would they trust you to support them to get over other obstacles that are in their way?

Concern 2: "I don't have the time."

This really means: *"I'm not making this a priority...yet."*

Here are 5 Magic Questions that will help your potential client discover if the result that you're offering is really a priority in their life or not.

Magic Question 1: *"Can I ask you a question about that?"*

Magic Question 2: *"If I waved a magic wand that created plenty of time in your schedule, is this something you would want to move forward with?"*

Magic Question 3: *"In order to say Yes to _____(the result they want), what would you have to say No to?"*

Magic Question 4: *"What would your life be like if you chose _____ (the result they want) instead of* _____*(what they just said they'd have to say No to)?"*

Magic Question 5: *"If you don't spend the time on* _____ *(the result they want) now, how is this going to affect you in the future?"*

Concern 3: "I need to think about it."

What this really means is *"I am afraid I will regret making this decision."*

It could also mean that they don't want to reject you or don't want to have to explain why your services are not a match for them.

So the key is to be sensitive to how interested they seem.

If they seem to be interested in your services, here are the 5 Magic Questions to support you to dance gracefully with this concern.

Magic Question 1: *"May I ask a question about that?"*

Magic Question 2: *"What else do you need to know in order to make your decision?"*

Often you'll find that they need to talk with their husband or wife, or they need to know they'll get a certain result out of the program. This will often help you answer questions that didn't get answered before.

Magic Question 3: *"How long can you go before you need to make this decision?"* or *"When do you want to make this decision?"*

You might find that the problem isn't urgent enough yet. Have you ever experienced a need creeping up on you and at some point it becomes urgent? You might find that, just by asking this question, the problem becomes more urgent more quickly to them.

Magic Question 4: *"What is the impact in waiting beyond x to make this decision?"*

What if they waited too long to make this decision? What if they stayed in the *"wait and see"* perspective.

Sometimes when our clients realize that if they don't make this decision right now, they may have to get a job, and that often makes it urgent and present enough for them to decide immediately.

Note from Sharla: At a recent Rejuvenate Your Practice 2 Day Intensive, I was having a Heartselling™ conversation with a woman who had gotten her education as a nutrition consultant over two years ago. She shared with me during the course of the conversation that she felt afraid to get started and she had been sitting on the fence for two years.

She was considering our Double Your Practice in 90 Days Program and told me she needed to think about it. Because we had a strong connection and I showed in service to her having what she wanted, she trusted me and gave me permission to coach her in this moment.

I invited her to consider what her future would entail if she said No to our program right now. And then I invited her to consider what her future would be like if she said Yes to our program. The choice to move forward and sign up for the program became very clear to her at this point where she had previously been stuck.

This freed a tremendous amount of energy as she joyfully said Yes.

Magic Question 5: *"What would need to happen for you to feel like doing (my service) was one of the best decisions you have ever made?"*

Sometimes people really do need to think about their decision and will feel pressured if you push too hard. Respect their process and then set up a specific follow-up time you both agree to (preferably within a week.)

At the same time, you may be someone who loves a lot of space to make a decision. You may tend to project that onto other people. The truth is that plenty of people make their best decisions when they're connected to someone and inspired, and giving too much space and alone time to make their decision will just bring them back into their head, which is filled with fear and doubt.

So, use your intuition and do your best to boldly serve people without giving them too much space and without pressuring them.

We suggest you keep this list of Magic Questions close to you and practice them, so that soon they will easily tumble out of your mouth.

PJ Van Hulle came to us as a successful real estate investor who wanted to teach other people how to invest, but didn't know where to begin. Through using the skills we teach in our Build Your Empire and Double Your Practice in 90 Days (or less) Programs, she earned 6 figures in her first year.

*Learn more about PJ at www.realprosperityinc.com

Recently, she shared with us that people come to her workshops and are interested in her amazing Real Estate Investing and Prosperity programs, but they often have concerns such as: *"How much does it cost?" "How much time will I have to invest to get results?" "Will it work for me?"*

Specifically, PJ shared one story of a woman who wanted to do her "90 Days to Your First Deal Program" but was traveling abroad for 3 months and couldn't make the schedule work.

Through PJ's ability to be of service to this woman (Earth Element), she heard what her potential client wanted and worked with her to discover a way to accomplish it. PJ worked out a special program for this client so she could get started right away with long distance learning and then fully jump into the program once she returned from her travels.

This woman said Yes to a lifelong dream of financial independence.

Here's what PJ said: *"The Heartselling™ skill I've used the most at my workshops is how to dance with concerns so I'm truly serving my potential clients to get what they want in their life... This skill alone is responsible for tens of thousands of dollars in sales and many lives changed for the better."*

You'll find that a lot less concerns come up when you go through all 6 Stages, because they'll see you as the solution to their problem. But if they're not present to the pain of their problem and how great your solution is, all kinds of concerns will come up because they won't be that hot for what you've got.

So, take the time to go through all 6 Stages. It's worth it. And when we share with you about packaging your services and creating programs, you'll be even more willing to have Heartselling™ conversations, because instead of spending 45 minutes with someone who is interested in a $75 session with you, you'll spend that 45 minutes talking with someone who is interested in a $500-$10,000 package or program you offer.

3 Secrets to Help You Dissolve Concerns

Secret 1: Stay Curious
In the space of a heartfelt, compassionate listener, concerns will dissolve, but only under one condition: You must listen and empathize, without believing that their concerns are true. By staying curious, you will be able to hear them without believing or disbelieving them. In this space of non-judgment, they will often shift from concern to empowerment.

Secret 2: Evoke Their Highest Commitment
In order to be effective with your potential clients, you have to help them get present to their highest commitment. Then, like any great coach, your job is to help them get anything that is in the way of their highest commitment out of the way. When their highest commitment becomes bigger than their concerns, they will say Yes.

Secret 3: Say Yes to <u>Your</u> Highest Commitments

Are you saying Yes to your Highest Commitments?

If your concerns around money and time stop you from taking the next step, your potential clients will feel it. You will be less effective in dancing with their concerns because it feels hypocritical to ask someone to take a step you're unwilling to take yourself.

There may be a clear next logical step for you to take. If you're taking it, great! If you're not, the reason you're not taking the next step in your own life and in your own business will most likely show up in your conversations with potential clients.

If you don't move towards your Highest Commitment because you don't think you have enough time or money, you are setting the precedent for your clients and they will reflect that same fear back to you.

For example, let's assume that you are deeply committed to getting more clients, and you feel that you don't have the time or money to attend a Rejuvenate Your Practice 2 Day Intensive. Even though we're offering you a Full Scholarship, perhaps you tell yourself you can't afford a plane ticket. Or maybe you say that you don't have the time to devote a weekend to practicing the principles that will help you become a client magnet.

That same lack of commitment to your own business will show up all over the place, because you let yourself get away with mediocrity, you'll let your clients get away with mediocrity. So, whether it's the Rejuvenate Your Practice 2 Day Intensive, or something else, we encourage you to ask yourself the same questions we gave you to ask your potential clients.

"What would you need to get out of _____, to make it worthwhile for you?"

And then show up to get that result. It's nearly impossible to hold other people to greatness when you can't hold yourself to your greatness.

You've just learned how all 6 Stages of a Heartselling™ conversation work together. Now you can use both the 5 Elements and the 6 Stages to serve your potential clients.

17

How "Energy" Plays into Your Heartselling™ Conversations and How to Use it to Increase Trust

As a Holistic Practitioner or Coach you are probably very intuitive and receptive to energy. The last thing you want is for people to see you as a hard seller who wants to close the sale and win. You probably hate it when people pull their energy away from you.

The Push-O-Meter

We've created a scale called the Push-O-Meter. On the left side is Pushover. On the right side is Pushy. Most practitioners and coaches hang out on the pushover side of the scale.

Pushover   Pushy

This is tragic, because if you're a pushover and don't step into the Wood Element of giving people a choice, you are robbing people of your gifts. But at the same time, you don't want to turn people off with pushiness. Believe it or not, when your heart is open and you're truly coming from service, you have more permission than you think you have.

Now, if you're not so bold with people that they occasionally confuse you with a hard seller, then you're playing it too safe. Because as a Heartseller™, you've got to want them to get what they want so badly, even more than they do themselves. Imagine a parent who wants nothing more than that their kids be happy. That's the commitment you want to have as a Heartseller™.

When a parent gets attached to their kids being happy, their kids will feel it and resist. They may pull their energy away.

Likewise, your potential clients may pull away too. What you do after they pull their energy away is what separates beginning Heartsellers™ from master Heartsellers™.

Sometimes you want something for someone so badly. You know that if they were to work with you, the problem that's been nagging at them for years could be resolved. You want them to have the freedom from this problem and you start to get attached. And as you feel that attachment, you start to feel yourself become more pushy and you start to feel them resisting.

This is totally normal and a sign that you care about people and want them to have a great life. You wouldn't have devoted yourself to the helping profession if you didn't want to help as many people as possible.

You don't need to be afraid of feeling attached. Here's the secret. When you start to get attached, simply be transparent and admit it. Here's what you can say:

"I have to admit, I'm feeling a little attached to working with you. I really want to help you and I see how much you can get from working with me. At the same time, I only want you to work with me if it feels right to you, and it may not be the best fit for us to work together. Can we keep exploring this and see what we find together?"

And, if you leave a conversation with the uneasy feeling that you were too pushy, it's not the end of your relationship. You can call them to apologize for being pushy and reaffirm your appreciation of them and commitment to always leave them feeling better than you found them.

Whether they felt turned off by you or not, they will love your transparency and authenticity and they will remember that you made your relationship with them more important than "closing another sale."

> Action Step 10: Swing out and be just a bit more "pushy" than you are comfortable with in your next 10 Heartselling™ conversations.

The Lean-O-Meter

At any given time, your potential clients are either leaning in or leaning out.

We have another scale that we call the Lean-O-Meter. To experience the Lean-O-Meter, rub your hands together. Now place your hands so that they are six inches apart. Can you still feel the connection between your hands?

That's like the connection between you and your potential client. As your connection gets stronger, they will lean in to the point where your fingertips are touching. At the same time, you may say something that decreases your connection. It may be unintentional, but the crazy thing about human beings is that you never know what will trigger them and have them lean away.

So, instead of playing tug-of-war with potential clients, as a master Heartseller™ you dance with your potential clients and increase the lean-in.

The Lean-O-Meter is always shifting. The 5 Elements will help you continually increase the lean-in and reduce the lean-away.

When you ask them what they're looking for, their answer will have them leaning in toward you.

Then you acknowledge them, and now their eyes are tearing up and they're leaning in even more. You tell them you can help them, and you share what you do. They're so excited, and they ask you how much you charge.

When you share that with them, you can feel them contract and lean away from you.

How you respond to your potential clients when they lean away from you will determine how successful you are as a Heartseller™. Instead of blaming yourself or thinking that something is "wrong," just remember that leaning in and leaning away is as natural in a Heartselling™ conversation as breathing in and breathing out.

When you feel the lean-away, simply choose the Element you want to stand in.

You can get curious with them by first sharing, *"I noticed you just seemed to pull away. What's going on for you right now?"*

For some people, just getting curious with them will be enough to bring the lean-in back.

Other people won't lean in until you step into the Metal Element and acknowledge them.

Or you may step into the Fire Element and laugh with them.

Or you may step into the Wood Element and challenge them.

Or you may step into the Earth Element and ask, *"How may I support you?"*

What's funny is that any one of these Elements may create even more of a lean-away. And because most people are more comfortable with some Elements and less comfortable with others, you'll never know until you're present in the moment with the potential client in front of you.

The number one key to Heartselling™ is to pay more attention to the lean-o-meter than anything else, including closing the sale.

This means that you have to be willing to dance from Element to Element to create more lean-in. And as you get more masterful, you'll become more intuitive about which Element to step into to create a stronger lean-in.

Let's say you say something that feels a little pushy. And you think, *"Maybe I just overstepped my boundaries."* You can use any of the Elements to bring the connection back into place.

And if you take anything away from this chapter, take this away: unless you have a strong lean-in, please, please, please, don't ask them to take the next step.

In other words, the only time you ask them to take the next step, whether it's a follow-up conversation, a complementary session, a workshop, a paid session, or a package, make sure that you have a strong lean-in.

Otherwise, it's like leaning in for a kiss when your date is leaning away, and then wondering why they turned their cheek.

But when the moment is right and they're leaning in, that's the best time to go for the kiss. Because people love purchasing services from people they feel connected to.

So, as a master Heartseller™, you make the Lean-O-Meter more important than "closing the sale." In doing so, you're on your way to building long-term relationships. So, even if the person you're talking to is not going to become your client, they will be more likely to refer people to you if they feel a strong connection with you.

18

Sample Heartselling™ Conversation

This is a transcription of a real Heartselling™ conversation that happened at a Rejuvenate Your Practice 2 Day Intensive.

> Action Step 11: Listen to the audio recording of this conversation at www.RYPScholarship.com between Sharla and Jan and make notes about which Element Sharla is using and which Stages she is in during points of the Heartselling™ conversation.

Sharla: It is nice to meet you, Jan.

Jan: Nice to meet you too. It is good to be here with you.

Sharla: Thanks for coming up, Jan. Tell me a little bit about what you do.

[Jesse's Commentary: Notice how Sharla creates an instant connection with Jan from the moment she starts talking with her, by being interested in Jan.]

Jan: I teach the art of tantra yoga.

Sharla: So we have actually met before, I think.

Jan: Have we really?

Sharla: Yes, I think we met; do you live up in the East Bay?

Jan: I do. I live in Berkeley.

Sharla: So we actually met at a Charles and Caroline Muir workshop, just briefly. I thought when I saw you that I recognized you and I have even been to your website and seen some of the things that you do.

Jan: Fantastic. What a coincidence.

Sharla: It is so nice to have you here.

Jan: Thank you.

Sharla: So how are things going?

Jan: Things are going pretty well, and they could be a lot better, and I am looking forward to seeing that happen.

Sharla: Tell me a little bit more about that…

[Jesse's commentary: Notice that Sharla invites Jan to share a little about what could be different and Sharla immediately asks her to share more about her challenges.]

Jan: About how the business is going?

Sharla: Yes.

Jan: I am really clear that this is my life purpose, so it is good to know that, and I don't have as many clients as I would like to, I would like, the workshops seems like a lot of effort to fill workshops and to enroll people in my work.

Sharla: If I remember, because I have been to your website and learned a little bit about your work, if I remember, you do both workshops and you do one-on-one work and couples work, and you go really deep with people and you also do the bigger picture with people, and can I share something with you that I noticed?

[Jesse's Commentary: Notice that Sharla lets Jan know how they have met before and Sharla took an interest in Jan's work knows something about her. Then she asks for permission to share something with her.]

Jan: Yes, please.

Sharla: You have a really bright spirit, and when I met you, you may or not remember but I really enjoyed meeting you. There is something, you are different, your energy is bigger, I feel like I get more of you now.

Jan: Oh great, that is good to hear.

Sharla: You have grown a lot in the last couple of years......

Jan: Yes I have grown a lot since then.

Sharla: I feel like a warm real connection instantly with you

[Jesse's Commentary: Notice how Sharla authentically acknowledges Jan.]

Jan: Do you know why that is?

Sharla: Why is that?

Jan: It is because of the daily Ipsalu Tantra practice that I do.

Sharla: Which is fantastic, because there you are -- you are actually showing the benefits of your work.

Well, that is beautiful. It is great to notice what a fun coincidence to see that change. So can I ask you a little bit about your workshops?

[Jesse's Commentary: Notice how Sharla uses her intentional curiosity to turn the conversation back toward Jan's business. And again, she asks permission. You can also feel how Jan and Sharla are connected with each other and Sharla now has permission to ask to hear more.]

Jan: Yes, of course.

Sharla: So, you are having a hard time getting people there and you said it is a lot of effort – can you tell me a little bit about that?

[Jesse's Commentary: Notice how Sharla continues to ask questions to encourage Jan to open up and share more about how her business is going here...because Sharla helps people with business, she'll always re-direct the conversation towards helping Jan in her business]

Jan: I do not think it is because I am putting in so many work hours. It feels like an emotional and psychological effort. It always happens but not without a toll to my emotional state. It feels very draining to do. It is not fun. I wish someone else would fill my workshops.

Sharla: I get that, I get that yes. Can I ask you a little more about that?

Jan: Yes.

Sharla: What is the drain, what is that, what is it about?

[Jesse's Commentary: Notice how Sharla is encouraging Jan to go deeper and deeper into the challenge she is dealing with.]

Jan: There is a feeling of going uphill or going against the grain, maybe a feeling that, let's see, that it is just going to be work to enroll people. It is not even a reality. It is just a feeling.

Sharla: Yes, Yes, so it is just that feeling of going uphill, and then I am curious, when they do get there, how is the workshop for you? Do you enjoy the facilitating?

[Jesse's Commentary: Notice how Sharla acknowledges the feeling Jan just expressed, with "it is just that feeling of going uphill," and then she asks another question for clarification. She asks a closed-ended question here, "Do you enjoy the facilitating?" helping Jan get present to the part of her business that she loves and why she does the other part.]

Jan: I love that part.

Sharla: You just wish someone else would take care of the marketing and the registration.

Jan: Yes, I'm still working on overcoming some fears, that is part of it, that is where my love is, where you feel most self-expressed and full of life.

Sharla: Yes, I can see that, you have that energy of I like. I can tell you have done a lot of work on your own charisma and having more of it, and you have a lot of it to share with the people on the stage.

[Jesse's Commentary: Another acknowledgment. Sharla lets Jan know she sees her power.]

Jan: Thanks, that is good to hear.

Sharla: Yes definitely, you have workshop leader energy. Which for me means somebody who has done a lot of work, is really self-expressed and shows a lot of life. There is a lot of life energy moving through you.

[Jesse's Commentary: Deepening the acknowledgment.]

Jan: That is great.

Sharla: Yes, so I am curious, it sounds like you love being on stage or in front of the room or in the circle or however it is that you do it, but the marketing or registration portion of it is a drag.

> You know there is some fear there. I am wondering, what if you could get over some of those fears?

[Jesse's Commentary: Notice the "what if..." question here. Sharla is supporting Jan to start dreaming into what it would be like to overcome this challenge.]

Jan: That would be great and I think people would like that too. I think when people do engage with me they have a positive experience.

Sharla: It is almost like they are going to have a better experience and so will you if you just get over some of these beliefs.

Jan: I really feel that.

Sharla: I am also curious, what if you had some tools that not to just get over the fear but to make the process a lot easier and to fill your workshops much easier...?

[Jesse's Commentary: Another curious "what if..." question to help Jan go deeper]

Jan: That is what I am here for. It would be a great relief.

Sharla: So it would make the process easier and get over some of those beliefs.

[Jesse's Commentary: Sharla is reflecting back to Jan what she is hearing so Jan knows she is totally with her and understands what she is going through]

Jan: Yes.

Sharla: Well if I could help you with that, would you be interested in hearing about it?

[Jesse's Commentary: This is a key turning point in the conversation. After talking with Jan and discovering the challenge she is dealing with and then inviting her to consider what it would be like if things were different, Sharla asks the question: "Well, if I could help you with that, would you be interested in hearing about it?" Sharla is doing a great job of creating the connection, being of service, acknowledging, and being curious. She has moved through the stages of Open the Conversation and Find out what Jan is looking for, and she is now about to Share a resource.]

Jan: Yes, like show me, show me, yes!

Sharla: Well, based on what you are telling me, we have a program that I would highly recommend, and it is for people who are either leading workshops or who are ready to or want to lead workshops, and we give you all the tools you need to lead really lucrative workshops and to make the process a lot easier.

[Jesse's Commentary: Notice that the resource Sharla is sharing is her program and how it is an authentic, heartfelt, and generous recommendation based on what she has heard from Jan so far.]

Jan: Tell me about it.

Sharla: It is called "Build Your Empire," and for us what we mean by empire is your heart-based empire; how do you want to see your world to be through your training, you know, the value people get from workshops? I mean you and I met at a workshop and here we are again, so you know the life-changing value that people can get from them, and you obviously believe in that as a way to make a change and help people in the world. And so it is about having the whole registration process be easier for you to be standing in your values so fully, that people are just so excited to say Yes to you. And we even give you all of our systems so that you can get somebody else to do your registration process if you want to, but it is good to get over your own fears. You want to be able to do that and be able to sell easily.

[Jesse's Commentary: Notice how Sharla is sharing about the program she has to offer and Jan is "leaning in." Sharla shares with Jan how the challenges she faces are exactly what Sharla can help her with.]

Jan: I want to master that process myself and then find people to do that for me so I can train them in the way that I know worked for me.

Sharla: Absolutely. There is another piece to it, can I share?

[Jesse's Commentary: Sharla is asking permission to share more, and you can feel that Jan is still leaning in because she is interested in hearing more]

Jan: Yes.

Sharla: So once you are at your workshops I would love to see you able to offer even more value than what you are doing at your workshop and here is what I mean by that – when people come to your workshop, there is so much more to get than from being with you for a couple of days in a retreat or whatever it is, and if they were to say yes to continuing to work with you how would that be?

[Jesse's Commentary: Notice how Sharla sees something greater for Jan than Jan has seen for herself. She invites Jan to visualize her workshops as being more than just a one-shot experience for her clients. Instead, the workshop is the start of a long-term relationship.]

Jan: Yes, that would be great. Although, I just heard a little limiting voice in my head that said: "*You will run out of things to say.*" Maybe they are enthusiastic to sign up for let's say a year's worth of coaching with me, but I might run out after 3 months and they have already paid me their money.

Sharla: So noticing that and what do you know about that?

[Jesse's Commentary: Notice how gentle and easy Sharla is with Jan's concern. Sharla continues to see Jan in her greatness and knows from her experience in working with so many people that what Jan is concerned about is not the truth. And notice how she gives Jan the space to look inside and question the truth about this concern. You can also hear that Jan is very self-aware, calling it a "limiting belief," so hearing this, Sharla is coaching her to move through the belief quickly]

Jan: It is a lie.

Sharla: You know that you are always learning and growing and are one step ahead of everyone else – how long have you been doing this work?

Jan: For about 8 years, 7 or 8 years

Sharla: You know that you know 99.9% more of this work than anybody else and you know one of the other things is it is not just about the information that you teach but the experience that you give people and I know you have a lot of tools for that

[Jesse's Commentary: Here Sharla is giving Jan value and real tools by offering her a new perspective about what Jan has to offer. She is foreshadowing some of what Jan will get in the program by giving her valuable information right now. And all of this is an acknowledgment of the work Jan has done so far.]

Jan: You know, you are right. I could lead someone through the same process over and over again for 12 months and they would continue to deepen and continue to get something out of it. Well, what a great realization!

Sharla: Absolutely. So I would love to help you do that, I would really love to see you make a bigger difference and help a lot more people and make a lot more money.

[Jesse's Commentary: You can hear Sharla asking Jan to take the next step in a very soft way here. You can see how Sharla isn't trying to "close the sale" but instead is helping to "Open Jan up" to Jan's higher commitment and then leaving the 'space' open for Jan to step into this higher commitment.]

Jan: Yes, it would help a lot of people make more money?

Sharla: No, you help more people and we help you make more money.

Jan: Help me make more money. Yes, that is the
                Vision I hold, that would be a dream...

Sharla: Can I hear a little bit about that dream?

**[Jesse's Commentary: Sharla is encouraging Jan to go deeper
into the dream through her curiosity]**

Jan: Yes.

Sharla: Tell me what would you want? If you had your
                ideal workshop business, what would you want
                it to look like? It is fun to imagine...

**[Jesse's Commentary: This is so exciting. You can feel the
resonance as Sharla encourages Jan to really get into her
Vision for her business. You can also hear how much space
Sharla gives Jan to think about it and gives her time to
respond]**

Jan: Yes, it would be in beautiful locations where
                people could feel really good about themselves
                and open. Let's see, they would make great
                friends there.

Sharla: Like a community energy?

Jan: There would be a community spirit and people
            show up and feel like, God, this is what I have
            been waiting for all my life and here I have
            found it. Thank you.

Sharla: I so get that, I have a teacher that is like that for
            me, Jesse and I do, it is like that feeling of
            "Wow this is what I have been waiting for my
            entire life…"

**[Jesse's Commentary: Here Sharla relates to Jan's dream of
what people will get out of Jan's workshops and
acknowledges her.]**

Jan: The planet's going through big changes. And I
            really believe that this system, this path, Tantra
            Yoga Ipsalu, is a doorway for people to live life
            in a big way and be totally connected to
            themselves and their souls, that the
            consciousness is requiring of us to continue to
            move forward and feel good and fulfilled.

Sharla: I totally get that.

Jan: I just want that for people because it is easy to
            feel lost these days.

Sharla: It is like about becoming more of yourself and
            becoming a bigger expression of yourself.

[Jesse's Commentary: Here Sharla acknowledges she really understands what Jan wants for people through working with her and shows Jan that she really gets it]

Jan: Yes and discovering who you really are.

Sharla: So can I share something with you?

[Jesse's Commentary: Sharla is about to re-direct the conversation back toward Jan's business here, so notice how she asks permission]

Jan: Yes, please.

Sharla: My experience of learning to be a more successful and powerful workshop facilitator and being able to sell from the stage has been like a yoga. I have had to grow myself, I have had to get over beliefs, I have had to love people more, I have had to get over all this stuff that I make up about what is going on out there and really be present and I really take it as a spiritual path.

Jan: Yes, I can see that.

Sharla: So I would love that for you – another form of yoga.

[Jesse's Commentary: Again, this is a soft way of Sharla inviting Jan to say Yes to the program Sharla is offering and relating it back to what is really important to Jan and her values]

Jan: Yes and I so identified with what Jesse said earlier that a big part of a key to growing your business is learning the pieces that you don't know that you don't know and I just feel like it is going to be easy when I get those pieces.

Sharla: I have a good feeling about you, that you will just put it in place, you have a really strong consciousness about knowing where your limiting beliefs are, you and I just did a quick little work, a little bit of coaching and you said "*I do not need that one*" so I feel that you will just move really quickly.

[Jesse's Commentary: Sharla continues to see Jan's greatness and acknowledges her. Sharla also is sharing with Jan how she sees Jan will be very effective in the program]

Jan: Thank you. I feel that too.

Sharla: You are welcome. I am curious about the money portion of the Dream…

[Jesse's Commentary: Sharla is again steering the conversation toward the tangible result Jan will get from participating in the program by finding out more about what

Jan wants and seeing if it is a match]

Jan: Well, I was hoping you wouldn't ask me!

Sharla: Well, that is an interesting reaction.

[Jesse's Commentary: Notice Sharla doesn't resist the reaction Jan has, but instead acknowledges Jan's response and is curious about it.]

Jan: I was waiting for the "well here is the program for you and it costs 5000 dollars" and I go "I don't have 5000 dollars, I can't do it."

Sharla: I am curious before we even talk about the program I want to make sure it is a good fit for you and we do not get the horn saying "no, it is not a good fit". I am curious......

[Jesse's Commentary: You can hear Jan's money concern coming up here and notice how Sharla dances with Jan's money concern by setting it aside for a moment and saying, *"I want to make sure it is a good fit for you."* Because Sharla and Jan have such a strong connection with each other, Jan trusts Sharla and they continue to explore together.]

Jan: You are so cute....

Sharla: You are cute too. I am curious. You know your dream workshop business, what would it look like? How much money would you make? How many people?

Jan: Can you help me with some parameters? How much money would I make? How many people? I want to serve a lot of people but the nature of the work is deep and intimate and so that is where I get stuck. I want to help a lot of people but I cannot imagine doing what I am doing on a very large scale for more than 30 people, and that might be a limiting belief.

Sharla: Sure. Well, the truth is that we met at a workshop and there were 60 to 100 people there and it was deep work and it was really precious. Now obviously, with having a more intimate group you can sometimes go deeper. Can I throw something out based on what I am hearing?

Jan: Sure.

Sharla: So something that I see, Jan, is I can see you having a beautiful year-long program with about 30 people who go really really deep with you and spending as much as $10,000 to $12,000 for the year to do that work, get some retreats, and maybe do some one-on-one coaching.

Jan: It brings tears to my eyes. I would never have thought of that possibility for myself.

[Jesse's Commentary: You can hear how moved Jan is by what Sharla sees possible for her. This is how a selling conversation is a healing conversation. Sharla is acknowledging that Jan is capable of creating so much more for herself than she thought was possible. The role of a Heartseller™ is to hold a bigger vision for the potential client than they do for themselves and this is beautifully demonstrated here.]

Sharla: I can see you helping a lot of people and having a really amazing 6 figure business, multiple 6 figure business very quickly.

Jan: I am done with those Nun past lives. I want to make some money.

Sharla: I get that, you are so ready. So Jan I would love to talk some more with you about this, I know that you are ready for this, I know if I use the word "dharma" to take this forward and to really have it happen and I know that I can help you with that and I have a call coming in in just a couple of minutes unfortunately...

[Jesse's Commentary: Sharla is letting Jan know that she believes in her and she wants to work with her. Sometimes you need to let your potential client know that YOU want to work with them.]

Sharla: I have a call that I have to get so I am wondering, can we schedule, can I actually call you back after this conversation I have?

[Jesse's Commentary: Here, Sharla is asking Jan to take the next step. Notice it would be premature to ask Jan to sign up for the program and there is more to explore here. So naturally, the next step is to continue the conversation at another time]

Jan: Yes I would love that Sharla

Sharla: This is about a 45-minute appointment, so can I call you back right after and we can talk a little further to make sure this is a good fit for you?

Jan: Yes, I would love that. Thank you so much.

Sharla: Fantastic, you are so welcome. We will talk very soon.

Jan: Ok, thank you for spending this time with me.

Sharla: You are welcome. Let's give her a big round of applause.

[Jesse's Commentary: The next day Jan and Sharla continued the conversation privately. Sharla danced with Jan's concerns until Jan felt clear about signing up.]

You can learn more about Jan at www.tantricjoy.com

NOTES:

PART II:

Powerful Heartselling™ Strategies for Creating a 6-Figure Practice

NOTES:

19

The Most Important Factor in Attracting Clients Instead of Chasing Them

Now that you've learned how to use Heartselling™ to have amazing conversations with potential clients so they practically talk themselves into working with you, we'll share the single most important factor to help people know exactly who to refer to you, have word about you spread quickly, and become known as the expert in your field.

This one concept is the foundation to all that you do in your business. Without it, you'll continue to chase clients. With it, you'll easily attract all the clients you want. It will be simple to create a business that brings you 6 figures or more and you'll always know what to deliver. You'll become the go-to person in your field.

When we discovered this concept, our business went from serving 50 clients in 2004, to serving over 200 clients in 2005.

We chose a niche.

Why is having a niche crucial to your business? Because when you don't have a niche, you are marketing to everyone. And when you're marketing to everyone, you're actually not marketing to anyone.

Did you know that the average person is exposed to 30,000 marketing messages per day? To stay sane, we tune most of them out. We only pay attention to the message that we feel will most serve us.

So, what's a niche?

A niche is a specific group of people with a specific urgent problem.

First, we'll tell you what happened in our business when we stopped marketing to everyone and instead focused on a specific group of people with a specific urgent problem.

We used to lead a workshop called "Fire in the Heart." It was an amazing, transformational workshop. And we only charged $75 for it. But we didn't have a niche, so trying to get people to sign up for this one-day, life-changing workshop was like herding cats.

Our biggest workshop, which we spent 2 months trying to fill, had 8 people!

Then, one of our mentors told us that the most important thing we could do to get our business growing quickly was to choose a niche.

At first we resisted, because we thought that choosing a niche would limit us. We wanted to transform the world! And we thought we would get bored if we just worked with one type of client.

After we got over our concerns, we chose the niche of Holistic Practitioners and Coaches. Why? Not only because we could solve a problem of not having enough clients, but also because most of our friends and clients were practitioners, we knew how much we enjoyed working with this group of people. And we understood how they think, what they buy, and where they spend their time and money.

Instead of leading the same Fire in the Heart Workshop, we asked our Holistic Practitioner and Coach clients and friends what they were looking for.

What we discovered was that most of them were great at what they did but were struggling to build their practices. So, we decided to turn our Fire in the Heart Workshop into a workshop that was transformational, heartfelt, and would help people build their practices. That was the day the Rejuvenate Your Practice 2 Day Intensive was born.

Because we now had a niche where we were working with a specific group of people and solving an urgent problem for them, magic happened. We went from leading a workshop of just 8 people to registering 94 people at our very next workshop.

That weekend we changed a lot of lives and made over $33,000. This was the weekend our company was born.

It took courage to choose a niche. But since that time, thousands of practitioners and coaches have gone through our weekend and have taken our other programs.

And the great thing is that they tell their friends. Why? Because another cool thing about having a niche is that the people in your niche know other people just like them. Take a moment and ask yourself: *"Who do I know who is a holistic practitioner or coach?"* Chances are you know at least a few of these folks. If you have a good experience with us, you'll naturally want to refer your friends to us.

And so it will happen for you, once you choose your niche. This is part of the 6-Figure Formula. During the first 2 years after choosing our niche, we made over $500,000 at our workshops alone. In our third year, we made almost $750,000.

We're not sharing this to brag, although we are very proud of our numbers.

We want you to know that it's possible, and it doesn't have to take years and years. It starts with your niche, and it grows as you become better at Heartselling™. And it grows exponentially as you get good at leading life-changing workshops.

Why does choosing a niche create such spectacular results?

The 3 main reasons choosing a niche is crucial to your business success are as follows:

Reason 1: When you choose a niche you become the expert in your field. Because you have "specialized," you become known for the specific problem you solve.

Have you ever noticed that heart surgeons make way more than general doctors? But general doctors can help people with all kinds of symptoms, so shouldn't they make more? Well, let me ask you this: If you have a heart attack, would you rather go to a general doctor or to a heart surgeon? And would you pay good money for that heart surgeon's specialized skills?

Once you specialize and become the expert on the subject, your services suddenly become more valuable to people. People will seek you out and pay you more for your services. This is why you'll attract clients to you rather than chase them.

When you become the expert, people come to you for exactly what you offer, and it's much easier to help them say yes, because they arrive already wanting the solution you can help them with.

As you get known within your niche and start to see more and more clients in your niche, you will gradually become an expert. If you're worried about having to become an expert right away, don't. It will happen over time as people start to see you that way.

Reason 2: You virtually eliminate competition.

We are not saying that you eliminate people who are also offering the same services you offer, but you actually eliminate *the paradigm of competition.*

For example, if one coach specializes in helping young mothers organize their time and another coach teaches women how to transition from working in a corporation to starting their own business and working from home, there is no competition between these two. They can both be great coaches and refer to each other because they wouldn't even be going after the same clients.

We live in an abundant universe. When you choose a niche, even though you are no longer marketing to everyone, you'll begin to feel the abundance of referrals come in and it will be so obvious for other practitioners to refer potential clients to you if you have a niche.

Reason 3: Your entire business will unfold organically.

When you choose a niche, you will get information from your clients and potential clients including the language for how you describe what you do and how to package your services.

For us it made everything so easy, including our marketing language, our branding and our business model.

It was during our Heartselling™ conversations that we listened to the language our potential clients were using which had us understand their most urgent problem they faced. As we tested a new brand concept we asked our clients what they saw and took their feedback to tweak our visual marketing materials. As we've evolved as a company, we shifted how we run our meetings to create a culture that infuses all of our workshops based on how we've seen it impact our clients.

And for our niche, we offer a ton of value at low or no cost because we understand the financial constraints our potential clients are dealing with. All of this unfolded organically as we implemented new ideas and got feedback.

Do you see how having one niche allowed us to keep discovering how we could further serve our clients and go very deep with this group?

We'll share more about how to create a powerful business model in a chapter 23. Getting your niche and creating a winning business model are the two foundational pieces that make the difference between a 5- and a 6-figure business. So, make sure to take some time with the chapters that cover these topics and really go through the exercises. Don't underestimate the power of having a niche.

20

How to Overcome 3 Most Common Concerns About Choosing A Niche

What we find is that even when we share how powerful creating a niche has been for us, concerns come up for a lot of practitioners and coaches. So if you're feeling concerned, resistant to the idea, or doubtful in any way, you have a lot of company.

In fact, at one time, we shared your concerns.

When we were leading our Fire in the Heart workshop, we were competing with every other "Live the Life of Your Dreams" coach or workshop leader in California. And since California is the "Transformation Capital" of the world, we were competing with thousands of coaches who were offering similar results. Think about how many people you know offering transformational work!

When we chose our niche of helping Holistic Practitioners and Coaches, suddenly we were unique, and the paradigm of competition didn't even exist. There is hardly anyone else who offers what we offer specifically for this amazing group of people. And there is no one who offers the integrated combination of real financial business success and heart-based transformation the way we do.

Once we chose our niche, we asked our clients and potential clients what their biggest challenges were. They told us, *"Not having enough clients."* So we created the Rejuvenate Your Practice 2 Day Intensive and then the Double Your Practice in 90 Days Program, which provides additional Heartselling™ strategies and follow-up support.

After our first clients graduated from the 90 Day program, they told us that in serving more people and working harder, they were starting to burn out. They asked us, *"How can we serve more people and make more money without burning ourselves out?"*

The Leverage Your Genius Program was born out of that question. Most of the people in our first Double Your Practice in 90 Days Program signed up for our first Leverage Your Genius Program. In the Leverage Your Genius Program, we taught them how to create information products, like informational CDs or the book you're reading right now.

We also taught them high-leveraged marketing principles, so they could reach more people with less effort. We taught them how to shift from working one-on-one to creating a program that would serve more people in less time while offering even more value to their clients and making more money. And this made it even easier for them to attract clients.

But then many of them had another problem. They witnessed how we were getting 50 or more people to our workshops and making $30,000 to $40,000 in a weekend. They wanted to know our formula. So we created the Build Your Empire Program.

Even though choosing a niche was a tremendous breakthrough for us, and even though our most successful clients work within a niche, we find that many Holistic Practitioners and Coaches share three common concerns.

Concern 1: "I don't want to focus on problems."

We first heard about niche marketing at a 9-day business retreat. We kept hearing that a niche was a specific group of people with an urgent problem, and we were both totally resistant to the model of solving a problem. *"Don't they know about the Law of Attraction?"* I whispered to Jesse. *"What you focus on expands. I don't care what they say. I'm not going to focus on solving problems. I'm about expansion and transformation."*

We resisted it all week and when we talked with many of the seminar leaders about it, they told us that until we had a niche, we basically just had a hobby. Ouch!

Note from Sharla: At the time, I was about to offer my first program. So, I decided to test their theory and I chose the niche of Women in Leadership. I asked the amazing women who I wanted to join my program what their biggest challenges were.

I got feedback that they were experiencing problems like not having enough time, extreme stress, and feeling like they were living in a masculine world where it was difficult to stay true to their feminine self while being a leader. They felt scattered and were dealing with financial stress in their business. How could they get it all done with so few resources? So I geared my entire program and marketing materials to address these challenges.

Because I was helping them overcome their challenges (or solve their problem), most of the women I interviewed signed up for my very first Women's Leadership Program.

From that time forward, we've stopped resisting that people indeed have problems. And who are we to think they should be enlightened and just want to focus on expansion and possibility.

The truth is that we want to be in a state of enlightenment all the time and focus only on what is positive. Although we have plenty of enlightened moments and often feel very present in our lives, we still have urgent problems we want solved. And we're often looking for someone who can help us solve those problems.

Note from Jesse: My Dad has a very close friend who was resistant to all of the new age-y, self-help personal growth, kinds of things he tried to help her with.

It wasn't until she was in a situation where she had to have surgery and was afraid for her life that she was willing to listen to my Dad's advice. He offered her a CD set that provides guided visualizations to reduce the fear in people who are about to go into surgery.

It was the first "New Age" gift she accepted and it reduced her fear about surgery and decreased her recovery time.

One of our mentors, Dr. Rev. Michael Bernard Beckwith says, *"Pain pushes until vision pulls."* Fortunately, you can't make someone have a pain they don't have. For example, if you have more than enough clients and you're making 6 or 7 figures, there is nothing we can do to make you think that you need more clients.

But if you don't have as many clients as you like, our programs become much more enticing to you, because they help you fill your practice.

The problem of not having enough clients becomes the gate.

Wanting a solution to their problem is a strong enough reason for people to walk through the gate. And on the other side of the gate, we help you in ways you don't expect.

We call this "stealth transformation." Because in order to attract more clients you need new information, skills, and transformation. People don't always expect transformational exercises in a workshop about increasing your client base. But our clients love it and it is one of the keys to their business success because you can't grow your business if you're not growing yourself.

So, the key is to offer them what they want: a solution to their problem. And then give them what they need. And when you help them solve their problem and transform their life in the process they will send all their friends to you.

But, unless you're solving an urgent problem (like relieving back pain, weight loss, sleeping through the night, etc.) they probably won't even see the gate. And if they don't see the gate, how can they walk through it?

Your job is to help them walk through the gate.

What are the most urgent problems you solve?

> **Action Step 12:** Brainstorm the urgent problems you can solve for your clients. Choose one (or a set) of problems that are related.

Concern 2: "I like the challenge of treating many different kinds of people. I don't want to get bored with just one kind of client."

When you dive into the Water Element, you explore the power of curiosity. What we have found is that when you are in a state of unadulterated curiosity, every human being you connect with is fascinating and so unique and inherently interesting that it is absolutely mind-blowing. So, if you think you'll be bored, we encourage you dig deep into the Water Element and get curious.

Concern 3: "If I specialize, won't I limit myself or the Universe from sending me clients?"

This is a great question. Strangely enough, when you narrow your focus, you get even more clients. The Universe responds because you are specific about your request.

Here's an example:
Any good fisherman will tell you that if you want to catch a fish, instead of trying to catch any and all fish, choose the type of fish you want, then go to the part of the river where your fish hang out, and offer them the bait that most entices them.

The same holds true as you "fish" for clients. Find your specific fish, and offer the most enticing solution to their biggest problem. This helps you focus since you most likely don't have unlimited time and money to devote to your marketing efforts and Heartselling™ conversations.

And the wonderful thing about choosing a niche is that, although you focus your marketing time and dollars on a particular group, it isn't necessarily the only type of client you work with. If you re fishing and you catch a fish you weren't intending to catch, you don't have to throw it back.

Note from Sharla: When I offered my first Women's Leadership Program, I was still open to working with one-on-one coaching clients. I was coaching 2 men, while the rest of my clients were in the women's program.

These men were executives in their businesses and did not care that my business card was orange and yellow or that my website had a curvy, feminine feel to it. We felt a connection, they wanted me to be their coach, and so we worked together. Even though my "bait" was geared toward women in leadership, they bit anyway. And we created amazing results.

Instead of going wide with your clients, you go deep with one specific group. And the very cool thing about this is you don't need to see everyone. As long as you have a niche that has several thousand people, and as long as you can serve a small percentage of these people, you'll have a thriving business.

So, who is your specific fish? Who are the specific clients you would most love to serve? What is your hook and bait? In other words, what urgent problem do you solve for them? When you are truly solving an urgent problem for a specific group of people, getting into their mindset and using their language, your business will explode and clients will come ready to say Yes to what you have to offer.

NOTES:

21

How to Know When You've Got a Good Niche so You Can Easily and Effortlessly Create Marketing Materials that Inspire Them to Say Yes

Once you choose a niche, you've got to make sure you've got a good one. You'll know you've got a great niche when people know **exactly** who to refer to you.

We call this The Face Rule.

When you share what you do and the problem that you solve, it's very important that people's faces come to mind.

For example, if you help people with back pain, chances are that when you speak with people about that, they will know exactly who to refer to you because the faces of people they know will come to mind with that problem.

If you help people who are going through divorce, we may know some people right now who could use your services.

If you help people who are struggling to find their soul mate, there are people out there who we could refer to you.

This is the power of choosing a niche, because people will know exactly who to refer to you. If you try to help everyone, it will be hard for others to know WHO to send your way.

Often just looking at problems you've overcome in your life will give you a clear niche. Many of our clients have used their own triumphs with past challenges and what they've learned through the process to create dynamic programs that helped others follow in their footsteps.

One of our clients Bella Shing* chose the niche of spiritual women looking to find their life-partners. She had been through a series of boyfriends over the years and none of them were her true beloved. Then she met Drew and everything changed.

They fell deeply in love and are now engaged to be married.

When we first started working with her, she wanted to teach principles on manifestation but was unclear about her niche because she knew she could teach people how to manifest anything. We urged her to commit to a niche through our programs and coaching, so that it would be clear that she was solving an urgent problem that spiritual women wanted solved. With some hesitation, she created her business around this niche of helping spiritual women find their beloved and quickly built a 6-figure business.

Having a niche was crucial to the clarity and attractiveness of her marketing message and filled her workshops.

Here's the big test of whether you have a good niche. When you share with other people your thoughts about who you can help and the urgent problem you solve, faces of real people should come to mind. If no faces come to mind, then you don't really have a good niche and you need to narrow your niche.

Warning: Most Holistic Practitioners and Coaches want to work with people who are "already on the spiritual path." The niche they choose is often spiritual people or people who have taken some steps along the spiritual path to help them take the next steps or to help them move through blocks or barriers to connect them with Spirit.

* To learn more about Bella visit www.ManifestingYourBeloved.com

Claim Your **Full Scholarship** to the Rejuvenate Your Practice
2 Day Intensive www.RYPScholarship.com

That would be a fantastic niche in a place where there's not much spiritual, new age, or personal growth activity. But in California or other major cities, where there is tremendous interest in spiritual and personal growth, that is the worst niche to pick because it's not specific enough and everyone else is going to pick that niche and everyone else is going to be speaking to those people.

Instead of marketing to and seeking out people who are already "on the path" and competing with everyone else who is seeking out those people, why not seek out people who don't have as much access to the spiritual path. And by solving a problem for them you will actually create a gateway for them to come in and experience your services, and you will be way more profitable as well.

Once you choose your niche, the next step is to interview people in your niche to find out their specific language so you can easily and effortlessly create marketing materials that inspire your potential clients to say yes.

How to Interview Your Niche

Step 1: Choose 10 people (current clients/potential clients) in your specific group of people.

Step 2: Focus their attention on the urgent problem you solve.

Here are some great questions to ask them:

- What is the urgent problem you solve?
- What are your biggest challenges?
- What are your biggest concerns?
- What worries you?
- What are you most proud of?

- What excites you?
- What frustrates you?
- What do you wish would just go away?
- What do you want more of?
- What do you think would help you get it?
- On a scale from 1-10, how motivated are you to have that?
- What's the maximum amount of money you would spend to have that?
- What's the maximum amount of time you would spend to have that?

Action Step 13: Set up phone appointments with potential clients or current clients in this niche. Tell them, *"I'm revamping my marketing materials and I really value your opinion. Would you be willing to spend 20 minutes on the phone to answer a few questions?"*

Most people will say Yes, because everyone loves to give advice. Ask these questions of your potential clients and write down the answers. Some of these interviewees might even become clients.

Conducting these interviews is a very powerful tool and will help you craft an effective answer to the question, *"What do you do?"* which is the subject of the next chapter.

22

How to Answer the Question *"What do you do?"* so Your Potential Clients Can't Wait to Hear More

Now that you've learned that a master Heartseller™ solves a problem for a specific type of client and you've interviewed members of your niche, let's create your answer to the question *"What do you do?"* so people can't wait to hear more.

The key to creating a hot answer to the question, *"What do you do?"* is to instead imagine they are really asking *"How do you help people?"*

Why? Because people don't really care about what you do. What they are interested in is the problem you solve or how you help people. So you're going to imagine, from here on out, that *"What do you do?"* really means *"How do you help people?"*

Then you can phrase your *"What do you do?"* statement in a way that is about serving others instead of making it about you. This will make your *"What do you do?"* statement much more compelling to them.

Here are some examples:

If you asked us *"What do you do?"* we would say, *"You know how there are a lot of holistic practitioners and coaches who really love what they do, but aren't making as much money as they would like to make? Well, what we do is teach them how to earn 6 figures in their business without compromising their values."*

If you asked our client PJ *"What do you do?"* she might say: *"You know how there are a lot of professional women home owners who are going to retire in the next 20 years but haven't saved enough money? Well, what I do is teach them how to turn their current assets into a money creation machine, so they can have financial independence."*

Do you see how each of these answers does not actually answer *"What do you do?"* but answers *"How do you help people?"*

Before you get started on your own *"What do you do?"* statement, it's important to understand how to evaluate your *"What do you do?"* statement so you can coach yourself to create a HOT *"What do you do?"* statement.

Here are some tips for evaluating your "What do you do?" statement:

- Is the language simple enough (you want a 7-year-old to understand what you're talking about)?
- Is the problem clear?
- Are the benefits hot?
- Are you intrigued or compelled to hear more?
- Do faces of people who could benefit immediately come to mind?

If the answers to these questions are all "Yes," this might be a HOT "What do you do?" statement.

If you didn't answer YES to all of these questions, here's how to evaluate the statement and some questions to ask to improve it:

- If the language isn't simple enough, what would make it simpler?
- What would make the problem clearer?
- What would make the benefits hotter?
- What would make it more intriguing?

- If no faces come to mind, is it because that type of person isn't in your community or is it because they are too vague about the person they are trying to reach? Can you think of another way of expressing who they want to reach so it could be a niche?
- What would make it more compelling?

Go and talk with the people you interviewed in your niche and get their opinion on how hot the statement is.

Don't worry about making it perfect. We've been honing ours for years and only recently landed on something that feels totally true and exciting to share.

Action Step 14: Share your *"What do you do?"* statement with 5 people. Tell them you are working on speaking more powerfully about what you do and you want their opinion. People love to give their opinion and will probably be glad to help. Then ask them the evaluation questions and be open to their feedback.

If they answer No to any of the questions, thank them for their valuable feedback and ask them what you could say that would have them say Yes to the questions. And if they say Yes, you might even get a client.

We recommend talking to people you don't know well for this exercise and ask them to be honest with you and be gentle with yourself. We honor your courage in stepping out and vulnerably sharing, even though you might not have it perfect yet.

Answering the question *"What do you do?"* is like inviting your potential client to walk through a gate with you. The problem that you solve is the gate. On the other side of that gate is where you get to transform their life, make a difference, and really support them.

Remember, it's called "stealth transformation" If they don't walk through the gate, you can't make a difference with them

If they don't seem interested or they say *"Interesting..."* but you can tell that they're not interested, then that means they didn't walk through the gate with you. If they're not intrigued and hungry to hear more, then you've got some homework to do on your statement. Keep getting feedback until people can't wait to hear more.

23

How to Choose a Lucrative Business Model to Create a 6-Figure Practice

If you're going to have Heartselling™ conversations that take your valuable time, wouldn't you rather have a conversation for a $1,500 package or a $4,000-$10,000 program than a $100 one-time session?

Imagine offering a $10,000 program and only needing 10 clients a year to earn 6 figures…wouldn't that be amazing?

Now, you may not be ready to take the leap to offer a $10,000 package or program yet. But if you're still offering your services one session at a time, you're missing out on the huge potential to make a much bigger difference with your clients and make a lot more money.

So we'll share our favorite strategies to dramatically increase your income by choosing a lucrative business model.

Most practitioners and coaches we meet aren't comfortable asking for a handsome fee for their services. But this isn't just about raising your fees; it's about finding a way to offer more value to your clients.

Would you like to know how you can increase the value you offer to your clients so you can sell high-ticket items?

Imagine what it would be like to offer your services for $1,500, $3,000, $5,000 or $10,000.

How would it feel to charge this much? Who would you have to become to stretch into charging this? How much value would you offer to your clients to stretch into this next level? The next 3 strategies will give you access to how you will be able to increase the value to your clients so you can charge this much....and how you can reach an income of 6 figures or more.

Strategy 1: Packages

Would you agree that if someone were to work with you for a minimum of 10 sessions, they'd get way more than if they were to experience only 1 or 2 sessions with you? We would hope so.

This first strategy is to package your services so you can earn more money in your practice starting today. This is very simple to do and you can do this in just 3 minutes.

Instead of offering one session at a time, you sell your services as a package of one-on-one sessions.

One of our clients was offering his bodywork sessions one at a time when he started the Double Your Practice in 90 Days (or less) Program. At the end of each session with his clients, he would invite them to re-schedule.

We urged him to sell his services as a package of 10 sessions, rather than just one at a time. He created a package and a compelling reason for why 10 sessions was the number of sessions needed to solve the urgent problem for his clients. He had also just relocated to Santa Cruz and was starting his practice from scratch.

Within 30 days he sold over $10,000 worth of packages and nearly filled his practice. His clients were happy because they got a better price for their package of ten sessions than if they had just signed up for one session at a time, and they made a strong commitment to themselves by signing up for ten sessions at once.

What's great about offering packages is that you ask for the money up front (see disclaimer below) AND you have the security of knowing that your schedule will be full for a few months, rather than not knowing what's coming in next week.

DISCLAIMER about receiving the money up front: If you are a **CHIROPRACTOR, ACUPUNCTURIST, or NATUROPATHIC DOCTOR** check with your State Board for rules and regulations about charging upfront for packages.

If this client had just offered his services session by session, we guess that most of his clients would have only come to 2 or 3 sessions, which would have given him only 20%-30% of the income he actually made. Plus, he would have had to have a conversation every time the clients came in for a session, rather than focusing on the work.

Here are some recommendations about offering packages:

First, discount your package from your hourly rate. If you charge $100/hour for your one-on-one services, then we suggest you offer ten sessions for $795. Your clients save over $200 by choosing your package rather than paying as they go.

It's worth the discount for 2 reasons:

First, when your client first starts to work with you, this is the time when they are most inspired to get the results that your services promise. They are most hopeful and most likely to commit to themselves at a higher level.

When they commit to a series of sessions, they will be looking for the continual improvement over time and they know they have a series of sessions to work through whatever it is they are going through.

When they come in session by session, it is likely that just a few sessions into their work their life circumstances will get in the way of their commitment. Or they might get discouraged if they don't see the results right away.

The second reason is to save time. If you have to have a conversation with them every time they have a session, you're spending too much time selling and not enough time getting paid for your work. It's much easier to book the series and have the conversation about continuing at the second to last session of the series.

We recommend that you add bonuses to your package. Along with the discount, this gives your clients an even STRONGER reason to sign up for your package.

Here's a list of some of the bonuses we like to offer:

- Books
- Information Products
- CDs
- Reports
- Supplements if you're a health care practitioner
- Other people's time

One of our favorite bonuses is "other people's time." Ask friends or colleagues who can also help your clients but aren't in direct competition if they're willing to offer a complementary session or free workshop. These are the best bonuses because they don't cost you anything, they're of great value to your clients, and they help your colleagues build their businesses because you're sending them potential clients!

If you're also offering complementary sessions or workshops, your colleagues can add your complementary session or free workshop as one of the bonuses of their package.

Do you see how fun this can be?

For now, you can keep this simple phrase for selling your package in your back pocket:

"I charge $100/hr. If you sign up for my _____ package, you get 10 sessions for $795. How does that sound to you?"

You can model this and adapt it in any way you see fit. Just memorize it so you can share it with confidence!

Strategy 2: High-Value Programs

Most Holistic Practitioners and Coaches choose their modality because they love the work. And most coaching and holistic trainings are set up for you to work one-on-one with clients, following the traditional private practice model.

Even the first strategy we shared still lives inside this private practice model. While there is nothing wrong with the traditional private practice model and it can certainly be very satisfying, it is not the most efficient way to run your business.

If this is you, you are currently trading your time for dollars and when you do this, there will always be a ceiling to the amount of money you can make.

Note from Sharla: When I first started my coaching and acupuncture practice, I worked one-on-one with clients. I loved it. But when I calculated how much I could make working with individual clients, even with a full practice, I realized that I would never make more than $80,000/year.

Maybe I would have raised my prices eventually, but truthfully, most people working in the one-to-one private practice model don't raise their prices much, because it's just too easy for clients to compare what others in your modality charge.

Employees live paycheck to paycheck. Practitioners and coaches who have a one-on-one practice live client-to-client. No matter how hard you work, there is always a ceiling to the amount of income you can make.

What if, instead of working with one client at a time, you could work with 10 or 15 clients at once?

Imagine this… Instead of offering your services one-on-one, you provide more value, make more money, and make a bigger difference with more people…all while working fewer hours!!

When you shift from one-on-one to one-to-many, you have **unlimited potential** in the number of people you can help and the money you can make.

So, if you could work with your ideal clients -- and lots of them -- what are some possible ways of delivering your service in a way that will allow you to serve more clients while giving them more value? How do you make this shift?

Well, now that you know:
- Who your niche is

- What their urgent problem is
- What they want instead…

You create an amazing program that will help them get exactly what they want. A program is a combination of information, a service or a variation of your service, and support where you work in groups rather than just one-on-one with clients.

1. Your Information

Have you ever noticed you say some of the same things over and over again to your clients? Well, when you have a niche, you also will share the same information again and again.

While it may seem repetitious to you, what you might not realize is that the information you share is <u>so</u> valuable to the people in your niche! So the first step is to realize that you have valuable information to share.

The next step is to take this information and turn it into a process you can teach. Any information you share or any process you take someone through can be turned into a system your clients can learn and use for their own benefit.

When you take this information and turn it into a step-by-step system, you have just created something magical for your clients…a system they can follow, even when they're not in your presence.

> **Action Step 15:** Take a moment now and brainstorm some of the information you share with your clients regularly. Brainstorm at least ten pieces of information that you share with clients.

For example, did you know that there are millions of people who don't know the importance of drinking a lot of water every day?

Note from Jesse: Did you know that the most common reason people are admitted into the emergency room is dehydration?

Seven years ago, I didn't know how important it was to drink water and I didn't realize how dehydrated I was. As soon as I started to carry a water bottle around with me, I started feeling clearer and more energetic, and life didn't feel like such a struggle.

So, if you're a nutritionist, you may share why it's so important to drink water, how much water to drink based on a person's weight, and what the impact of not drinking water is, with your clients over and over again.

If you could share a process with your clients that they could do over and over again, even when they're not with you and it would help to solve their urgent problem, what would you share?

2. Your service or a variation of your service:

There are many options for how you can include your service in your program.

You can include in your program:

- One-on-one coaching (even if you're not a coach)
- Group coaching
- Tele-classes

- Coaching gym model
- One-on-one sessions of whatever your current service is
- Delivery of your one-on-one service in a group format

In case you're not familiar with the concept of the "coaching gym," it's this: Your coaching gym is open for specific hours during specific days of the month.

Your clients in your program can access the coaching gym for as little or as much time as they need. You can include this as "unlimited coaching" for your program if you would like.

Doesn't that sound valuable?

Even if you're not a coach, you can still offer some type of coaching, guidance, or support through having a "gym" as part of your program.

Note from Sharla: When I first started my coaching practice, I offered three 40-minute sessions per month for $300/ month for my clients. I had to work really hard to get those clients because there isn't much perceived value in three 40-minute sessions.

Then I created my first Women's Leadership Program and I offered information in the form of workshops and teleclasses and unlimited coaching. My coaching gym was open 15 hours per week for 3 weeks of the month and clients called in for coaching when they wanted it.

Doesn't unlimited coaching sound so much more valuable than three 40-minute sessions?

It did to my clients. I filled my first program with 9 women paying $400 per month. And I still had several one-on-one clients who weren't part of my women's program and I *scheduled them during my coaching gym hours.*

And the funny thing is that most women in the program only used about 2 hours of coaching per month, even though they had access to much, much more.

You can see how this coaching gym model allows you to provide so much more value. And it's got a high perceived value by clients. The truth is that most clients don't need more than one or two hours of coaching per month anyway, and they usually won't take advantage of more than that.

Many of our clients still choose to work one-on-one with clients, but only those who sign up for their program. When you are offering group work to share the information, you spend less time individually with clients, so they get great results with less of your time.

One of our clients created her first program while working with us. Before she met us, she was only working with clients offering one-on-one sessions.

Through our coaching, she realized that what delighted her most was to support women to lose weight naturally and without dieting. She had struggled with her weight as a young girl and was now a walking testimonial of vibrant health and great energy.

Since she now had a distinct niche, helping women lose weight naturally, it was time to shift the way she offered her services from one-on-one work to a program. She put together her information into different modules on effective weight loss. It included a workshop and some teleclasses to share her system with all her clients at once in the group.

She also felt it was important for her clients in this program to receive ayurvedic massage. So, two ayurvedic massages were included in the program each month. In addition, she wanted her clients to have group exercise time, so she included group time with a trainer.

By including the services of ayurvedic massage and personal training, she gave so much value to the clients in her program. She included supplements and a one-on-one health evaluation, to personalize the program for each client.

The most brilliant part of this program was that, although she delivered the initial health evaluation and the group classes with information about weight loss, she did not deliver the other one-on-one services but hired other practitioners to do the one-on-one and personal training services.

She was able to charge $500 per month for this 90-day program and was working with clients fewer hours than when she had a private practice.

She launched and filled her first program within 3 months of conceiving the idea and quadrupled her monthly income in less than 2 months.

Now there are other ayurvedic practitioners out there and there are other weight-loss programs out there, but there was nothing to compare her program to…it was amazing!

> **Action Step 16:** Brainstorm the ways you might like to offer your services to your clients to get them better results through your program.

3. Support

Some common forms of support include

- Buddies
- Homework parties
- Yahoo groups
- Online chat & networking forums
- Weekly emails

We love adding buddies and homework parties to our programs because our clients connect and bond with each other and gain so much value from being together.

To give you some ideas, here's how we offer support in our programs:

- **Accountability Buddies:** In the Double Your Practice in 90 Days (or less) Program we assign Accountability Buddies. This helps our clients stay connected with each other through the end of the program and offers them support when it gets tough.

- **Homework Parties:** In the Build Your Empire Program we have clients get together in Homework Parties. In this program, clients put together their workshop material and actually lead their workshops, so in the homework parties they get together to practice and support each other. In this way they are able to make more powerful offers so they can sell from the stage more effectively and stay connected.

- **Yahoo Groups:** In the Leverage Your Genius Program we have a yahoo group. We teach clients how to create and market their information products. The clients use the Yahoo group to share valuable resources like Lulu.com and Nolo.com.

- **Online Chat & Networking Forums:** In our 6-Figure Success Circle we have an Online Chat & Networking Forum for clients to post something they're looking for and to get replies to it.

- **Weekly emails:** Double Your Practice in 90 Days (or less) includes a short autoresponder email every week with a short homework assignment and a link to an online assessment, where clients can enter in how they did this.

What **forms of support** would best serve your clients to get the results they want to get in your program, *without taking your personal time and still supporting your clients?*

Action Steps 17 - 23:

17. Information: Decide what would be the best format in which to deliver this information.

18. Service: Decide what service you would like to provide in your program.

19. Support: Decide what forms of support you can offer to provide even more value to your clients in the program.

This will get you started in developing your programs. But in order to make it extremely lucrative, you've got to run the numbers for this new business model.

The following questions will help you determine whether this program will be a lucrative business model for you.

20. How many clients do you want in your program?

21. How much time will you spend delivering the group work and individual service?
_____ hours per week
_____ hours per month

Or how will you have someone else deliver the individual service, and for how many hours?
_____ hours per week someone else delivers the service
_____ hours per month someone else delivers the service

If you've planned it well, you should be spending less time delivering the work than you would have if you delivered all this information and service one-on-one.

22. How much will you charge for this program?
Consider the amount of time you'll spend delivering the program and the value you offer to your clients:
_____ hours per week
_____ hours per month

Consider the value you're offering: think about how badly they want this problem solved.

23. How much are you projected to earn from your first program? Multiply this number by the number of clients you want in your first program.

Tuition for the program = $_____ (A)
Clients desired in first program =_____ (B)
_____(A) x _____(B) = $_____

If you've planned well, you should be making more money than if you worked one-on-one with these clients.

When we created our first program, we simply modeled another program we had seen. They offered teleclasses, group coaching, one-on-one coaching, and a yahoo group. We did the same.

What's so great about offering a comprehensive program that includes information, service, and support rather than just one-on-one work? Not only are you no longer trading your time for dollars, but your clients no longer relate to their working with you by how much they are paying for the individual sessions with you.

This makes it nearly impossible to compare what you offer with what others in your modality offer. And the fun thing about this is that once you start creating your program, you'll uncover more information about your system and you'll continue to add more value as time goes on.

Your clients will help you fill in any gaps through their questions and you can continually increase the value and the price of your program!

Strategy 3: Always Offer the Next Steps

Studies have shown that it is much easier to continue to offer services to a current client than it is to get a new client. Once your client finishes your first series of sessions or your first program, they have a new dilemma, which is the next problem they're dealing with. Inherent in every solution is a new problem.

Here's what we've noticed. No matter what level of success or happiness we reach, there is always the next goal, the new set of issues that arise from not having been where we are now.

When we first started our practice we had a certain set of problems, which were mostly about not having enough clients.

When we solved that problem we then had to deal with not having enough time to service all our clients and needed a solution to that.

Then we figured out how to serve as many clients as will join us, but we had a team of 15 people who support our company and had to learn how to be effective managers in the business to keep the vision alive and the team inspired.

We also tripled the company revenue in our third year of business to almost $750,000, and with that type of high-growth company we had a whole new set of problems.

No matter where we've been in our business, we've had a set of problems we wanted to solve. Don't assume that because your clients have gotten the solution to one problem you've solved through your packages and programs that you cannot help them further. Your intention with your clients is to develop a long-term relationship with them and to continue to help them for as long as you can.

So the third strategy is to offer the next steps through an additional program or package. Whenever we are about to complete a program, we ask our clients, *"What do you need next?"* And they always give us the exact information we need to continue to deliver more value and support them in what they want next.

At a minimum, if you sell your services in packages, for instance 10 sessions at a time, you will dramatically increase your results.

And when you develop a program that offers more value to your clients while taking less of your time, you'll be well on your way to a 6-Figure Practice.

Lastly, continue to offer your clients the next steps, so they can stay with you long term. Ask them what they are looking for next as they are getting close to the end of their package or program, and then create it for them.

Remember, we said earlier that we've kept listening to our clients as well as Spirit. Listening to our clients has been responsible for hundreds of thousands of dollars in additional income. That's because we continually create the next program to support them in what they are looking for.

We now have 7 training programs. Our earlier programs give our clients the strategies to go from just starting out to earning $60,000/year. Other programs teach our clients how to create information products and leveraged programs to earn 6 figures and up. We've even got a program that helps a low 6-figure earner transition into making mid 6 figures.

We're solving different sets of problems with different programs, and as our clients move through one program successfully, they have a different set of problems that we help them resolve with the next program.

Now it's your turn.

After your clients complete their first program with you, what are the next set of problems they will deal with and how can you help?

NOTES:

_____

24

Leverage your Heartselling™ Skills to Earn a 6-Figure-Plus Income

Now that you understand how to use Heartselling™ to have great conversations with potential clients for very lucrative programs and packages, it's time to leverage your Heartselling™ skills to earn a 6-figure-plus income.

Earlier, we asked if you would rather have a Heartselling™ conversation for a $100 session or for a $1,500, $3,000 or even $10,000 program. Now we ask: *"Would you like to have Heartselling™ conversations for an influx of many clients all at once that bring you tens of thousands of dollars?"* Again, we hope you say, *"Yes, absolutely!"*

Once you gain mastery with Heartselling™ conversations with potential clients, it's time to take the quantum leap into using Heartselling™ to create great joint venture (JV) relationships.

What is a joint venture relationship? It's a relationship where one JV partner recommends the other JV partner to their clients and/or database and makes a percentage of the sales from that introduction. We often do this in an interview format over the telephone, where one of our JV partners interviews us on a free call about our area of expertise and then we make an offer for one of our products or programs on the call as a special deal for their clients.

To understand how profitable one of these calls can be, imagine you're selling a $500 product and 10% of the callers purchase the product. If you're offering a 50/50 split (meaning you take 50% of the revenue earned from the call and your JV partner who invited her clients to join the call gets 50%), you make $250 for every purchase. What if you had a partner who brought 50 people to the call? You could sell five products and make $1,250. What if you had a partner who brought 1,000 people to the call? You could potentially make $25,000 for one great relationship and an hour-long call! Once these people purchase the initial product or program from you, you can continue to offer them the next steps and earn even more money. And you can repeat this process with several JV partners.

You can also be the person who brings the listeners to the free call and earn thousands as an affiliate. Do you see why it's important to create great relationships with potential JV partners?

Recently, we were at a networking event with many of the world's top internet marketers, people with client databases of 200,000 or more people. We knew that if we could create great relationships with some of these folks, we had the potential to reach tens of thousands of potential clients and earn tens of thousands of dollars.

We were delighted when the man who created the event made an announcement, *"All right everyone. The questions are 'Who is your best customer?' and 'Who is your best partner?' Ask those questions of everyone you meet this weekend."* This set up exceptional networking for the entire weekend. Each conversation started with these two questions. And we walked away with new relationships worth hundreds of thousands of dollars in new clients.

What made the difference in our conversations? The questions the host recommended are Heartselling™ questions that we would ask any new person we meet at a networking event. After we asked those two questions, we used our Heartselling™

skills to connect, serve, acknowledge, be curious, and give them a choice. So, the very same skills you have learned for potential client conversations are the skills that will make you an incredible networker.

Our Heartselling™ conversations at the event with potential JV partners created the foundation of the relationship. At these types of events, you simply lay the groundwork with friendly conversation and genuine interest in what they have to offer. Then you discover together if what you both have to offer is a possible match for some type of joint venture or referral relationship, and then you make a commitment to follow up with each other.

Here's an example of how a conversation might go:

After introducing myself I ask: *"What brings you here?"* (curiosity)

He answers with how he was invited; we talk a little more about that (creating connection), and he asks: *"How did you get invited to this event?"*

I say, *"I was invited by Eben. We met through our mutual friend, Rose.* (We talk more about that) *So, tell me about your business; who is your ideal client and who is your ideal partner?"* (service)

He shares about how he coaches people to discover their ideal business by uncovering their genius.

"Tell me more about that." (curiosity)

He shares more about how he got into his current business and we get to acknowledge him for the mindset shifts he had to make to get to where he is now. (acknowledgment)

Then he asks, *"What about you? Who is your ideal client and who is your ideal partner?"*

I share a little about how we teach Holistic Practitioners and Coaches how to earn 6 figures in their businesses. *"We're looking for partners who can either put us on a teleclass where we can teach our Heartselling™ system or introduce us to coaches, holistic practitioners, and other heart-based business owners."*

He shares a little about how it might be a good match for him to share about our work as a resource for his graduates.

We find out that we live in the same area, so we finish the conversation with *"Let's have lunch to talk about this further. How does that sound?"* (give them a choice)

During the follow up phone call (you make within a week of meeting them), you remind them of your conversation, what you discussed, and say: *"I'd love to hear more about what you're looking for and share more about a great opportunity I have to offer so we can see if we've got a match."*

Using curiosity, you might ask questions like, *"So tell me what you're up to and what you're looking to promote right now."*

You'll listen to discover if what they have to offer would provide valuable content to your clients or email list. You may request to review the product/program they want to promote and see the sales letter or promotional material for the product.

We like to look at the opportunity to introduce them to our clients and see if it's a match for us to be introduced to their clients and/or database. The most important thing is to find a win-win situation and using your Heartselling™ skills will help you discover the most optimal partnership you can create.

25

How to use Heartselling™ to Lead Others to Support You in Your Vision

As your business grows, you'll need to become a leader: a leader to your clients, and a leader to your team. Your team may start with just a bookkeeper and a graphic designer. After a while, you may realize that you have more on your plate than you can possibly handle and you'll need to bring others onto your team.

For you, "team" might mean one assistant who takes care of administrative tasks. Or it might mean several other practitioners that work directly with your clients.

Your team is one of your biggest assets in your business. Without a team, you will always have a ceiling to the amount of income you can make. And without a team, you end up doing work that doesn't suit you and travel down the road to burnout. But a team that doesn't feel connected to the mission of your practice can fall apart quickly. And a team that buys into your mission to help clients and make a difference can raise you up and help you easily earn 6 figures.

How do you keep your team connected and happy? It is through Heartselling™ that the team members continue to feel excited to be a part of your business.

Imagine having a work environment where the members of your team feel connected and inspired to serve not only the clients, but each other. Imagine they acknowledge each other regularly, get curious when it gets tough, and make clear decisions to move forward quickly.

When you use the 5 Elements to connect, serve, acknowledge,

be curious and give them a choice with your team, you create a supportive environment where your team members feel like they're making a difference.

That's what happened to us. After hiring a bookkeeper and graphic designer, we hired an assistant. At first we were really bad at managing her. While we were teaching the Heartselling™ at our workshops we were forgetting to use it with our team member.

But as our team grew, we relaxed into our leadership and we found Heartselling™ naturally emerged. And because most of our business was running without us, we started to enjoy more time off. Instead of spending most of our day doing administrative work, we were able to spend most of our time writing and delivering content for our programs, coaching, and leading workshops.

You may have already hired an assistant. If so, this chapter will be essential for you.

If you haven't hired an assistant yet, and you are having Heartselling™ conversations, you will soon need an assistant, because your schedule will fill quickly.

You can start by hiring an assistant for 5-10 hours per week. By paying this person 12-15 dollars an hour you will have more time to do the things that will bring thousands more dollars into your business. And you'll have time to rest and rejuvenate yourself as well.

Hiring an assistant is like repotting a plant to a bigger pot. It allows your business to keep growing.

So, if you're growing quickly right now, or plan to grow quickly, learning Heartselling™ for leadership will support you to go to the next level.

Use the Fire Element for Connection

When you first hire an assistant, it may be a stretch for you financially. You're going to want to make sure that your assistant is "earning their keep and doing a great job."

If you hover over them and watch their every move, they're going to feel your heat a little too strongly. By micromanaging your assistant, you burn them with your fire.

But, if you give them so much space that they don't feel your warmth, they will start to get "cold feet." They will become easily distracted, unproductive and will most likely start doing their personal business while they "are on the clock."

The key is to connect with them regularly so that they feel your warmth, without burning them by crowding in to close. We recommend receiving short daily updates via email and then meeting weekly by phone or in person with your assistant to check in about the areas they are accountable for, and celebrate their successes.

Use the Earth Element for Service

Your assistant's job is to support you. The reason you are giving them your hard-earned money is to compensate them for making your life easier.

But if your assistant is not feeling supported, nourished, and nurtured by you and your company, they will most likely start looking for another job that offers more support.

At the same time, it's possible to give your assistants too much. If you spend hours and hours counseling them personally or if you're paying your assistants more than you're paying yourself, you are probably overextending yourself.

We recommend checking in with your assistant at your weekly meeting to find out how you can support them more fully. Then, support them as best you can, without draining your resources.

Use the Metal Element for Acknowledgement

There are studies that have been done that show that if someone is working hard and doesn't receive acknowledgement for their work within 1 week, they will start to feel unappreciated and resentful.

At the same time, if you acknowledge them in order to try to get them to work better or faster, your assistant will feel your manipulation.

So, it is important to acknowledge your assistant regularly. Take a moment, check in with your heart, and ask yourself: *"What do I appreciate most about my assistant right now?"* Then tell them what you discover.

Use the Water Element for Curiosity

One of the biggest ways your leadership is tested is when your assistant breaks an agreement or a deadline with you.

If you assume that they were at fault, you can damage the relationship. And if you ignore the fact that the agreement was broken, you are saying that it is acceptable to break agreements with you.

Instead of ignoring the situation or approaching your assistant with an accusatory tone, we recommend getting curious. You can say something like: *"Given the fact that you're always so responsible and dedicated to getting things done on time, I was surprised that you missed that deadline. What happened?"* This addresses the issue without blame and allows your assistant to respond without feeling defensive.

Use the Wood Element to Give Them a Choice

As the leader, you wake up every day and say yes to your vision, no matter how you feel. Your job as a leader is to inspire your assistant to say yes to your vision as well. If your assistant is not inspired to say yes to your vision, they will sabotage your success and their weak yes will become a no.

Now, you may feel that it's their responsibility to say yes, but really it's your responsibility to lead them in a way that they want to say yes.

If you boss them around all day, they will not take ownership over their responsibilities, and they will trudge through the day with a very weak "yes." But because they are feeling forced to say yes, their "yes" will turn into a "no."

At the same time, if you don't tell them what you want them to accomplish, they will most likely get distracted and bored. Because they have nothing to say yes or no to.

As the leader, it is your responsibility to set the results you need your assistant to produce. Then, allow your assistant to take ownership over those results. Once they take ownership, they are saying yes in a big way, and because they are more fulfilled, they will work better, faster, and stay longer.

You'll also have Heartselling™ conversations with your team members when you find that what you have delegated to them isn't turning out how you expected or they need someone to talk with about a difficult client interaction.

With your heart open and connected (Fire Element), you might ask *"I know how much you care about our clients* (acknowledgment) *and it's unusual for you to feel upset about a client interaction."* And then you move into curiosity, *"Tell me what happened."*

You listen generously and stay connected. *"I understand,"* you say as you continue to listen. *"I get it. It was a really tough conversation. Thank you for supporting the client to feel great about their work with us. Is there anything else?"* you acknowledge and remain curious.

"What can I do to support you in this?" you ask using the Earth Element of service.

"How would you have handled this differently if you could do it all over again?" you ask using the Wood Element to give them a choice so they can learn from what happened.

Once you start practicing Heartselling™ principles to lead your team, you'll find their loyalty and dedication to your clients will increase dramatically.

26

How to Use Heartselling™ During Your Workshops to Increase Back-of-the-Room Sales

Public speaking is said to be the highest paid profession in the world. We've personally had 6-figure paydays leading workshops and many of our clients have earned tens of thousands of dollars in just one weekend. Did you know that the biggest difference to make and the biggest money to make is not from checks received for speaking engagements? Instead, most seminar leaders make their money through back-of-the-room sales.

You've probably seen it before. You're at a big seminar and the speaker shares valuable information and then offers a program for a special price that day. Participants get up from their seats and head to the back table, where they sign up.

It looks like a dream, right? Well, it is a really amazing feeling to share about a program we believe in and see people headed for the back table. But what happens to the folks who go to the back table and still have questions or doubts. This is where Heartselling™ can make or break your speaking career.

There are speakers and workshop leaders who are so talented at selling from the stage that hoards of people run to the back of the room. But they didn't start out that way. Every professional speaker and workshop leader started out in smaller rooms when they didn't have as much talent or skill. They might have even started with rooms of 5 people.

Even with only 5 people, your workshop is the best place to have Heartselling™ conversations.

Why? There are 3 Reasons. At your workshop:

1) You're seen as the expert. They've just spent at least 2 hours learning from you so they'll take your services more seriously than if they just met you at Starbucks.

2) You're seen as a trusted advisor. As long as you deliver a valuable workshop and genuinely want to serve them, they're more likely to take your recommendations.

3) You save LOTS of time. Imagine your participants are inspired by what you've just taught them at your 2 hour workshop. But you know that if they keep working with you, they'll get even more value. So rather than starting from the beginning of a Heartselling™ conversation, most people will approach you with a concern.

So how should you handle this? With Heartselling™, of course. The same principles apply. Connect, Serve, Acknowledge, Be Curious, Give them a Choice.

The best thing about having Heartselling™ conversations with someone who has been participating in your workshop is that you've been having a conversation from the front of the room the entire time. The one-on-one conversation is actually a continuation of the Heartselling™ conversation you've been having with the whole group.

When a participant approaches you, you're already connected. A simple handshake and *"Tell me your name"* might be all you need to be fully connected. Usually, we find a participant starts with, *"I'm interested in program x, but I have this concern."*

We immediately say, *"Tell me what you're looking for,"* and the Heartselling™ conversation flows easily from there.

Next we might ask: *"What would you need to get out of program x to make it worthwhile for you?"*

And the participant might say, *"Well, I would want _____. And if I could get that, I would totally sign up for your package!"*

We tell her, *"Yes, you can get _____. And you can also get _____."* We feel her excitement and so we ask *"Would you like to sign up?"*

"YES!" she says.

Because most of your Heartselling™ conversations with participants in your workshops will be about dancing with concerns, you must master Stage 6 (Dance with Concerns). And because many new workshop leaders don't have this skill, they think free classes and workshops don't work and they give up.

So how can you use Heartselling™ to increase your back-of-the-room sales?

It's simple: be available during breaks to talk with participants. And train your back-of-the-room assistants to become masterful at Heartselling™ too.

No matter how masterful you become at selling from the stage, you will always increase the number of clients you'll receive by having Heartselling™ conversations with participants who still have questions.

What Should I Do Now?

We hope you enjoyed reading this book. But more important, we hope you use what you've learned to have Heartselling™ conversations with potential clients.

In our experience, however, reading alone will not make you a masterful Heartseller™. Reading is a good start, but if you want to get clients, you must actually have Heartselling™ conversations with real people.

In Part I of this book you learned about Heartselling™ basics. We suggest you practice using the 5 Elements and the 6 Stages in all of your conversations with potential clients. Notice if they are leaning in and if they lean out, use one of the Elements to bring back the lean in.

In Part II of this book you learned advanced Heartselling™ strategies to help you create a 6-figure practice. Using these strategies will increase the perceived value of your services and give your potential clients reasons to say yes more easily. If you choose a niche and create a program that supports that niche with the solution to an urgent problem, this will significantly reduce the amount of time you spend having Heartselling™ conversations as your offering will be more clear and compelling.

Even though we've given you incredible strategies for creating a 6-figure practice, most practitioners and coaches won't do it.

Why?

Because if your environment supports you to remain the same it is very difficult to make changes. And it takes a lot of courage to have Heartselling™ conversations. You must shift from shyly handing your business card to a potential client, hoping and praying they call to proactively connecting with people, showing up in service, acknowledging them for their brilliance, being curious about them and boldly giving them a choice.

To support you in using what you've learned in this book, we've provided you with several gifts. Be sure to visit www.RYPScholarship.com and pick up your FREE GIFTS that include:

- The audio recording of the Heartselling™ demonstration with Jan from the appendix of this book

- A printable poster of the 5 Elements and 6 Stages

- Your Action Guide for the exercises in this book

- Your subscription to the bi-monthly 6-Figure Practice Ezine packed with tips and resources to attract more clients and create a 6-Figure income.

As we shared earlier, we originally used Heartselling™ just to build our own private practices. But as friends and colleagues witnessed our rapid success, they wanted to learn how we were doing it. Since first teaching the Heartselling™ principles to our friends, we have been blessed to support thousands and thousands of practitioners and coaches to get more clients without compromising their values.

We feel strongly that the biggest difference to be made is by you, the holistic practitioner or coach, whose reason for being in business is to serve people to become happier and healthier.

And we want you to succeed, so we're excited to invite you to attend the Rejuvenate Your Practice 2 Day Intensive. This event will shift your beliefs about selling so much that you'll be wondering what was stopping you from talking with potential clients. You'll get the 5 Elements in your bones so you walk away feeling inspired and having real world strategies to get new clients immediately.

This incredible weekend will help you move past what has been stopping you in having the practice you've been dreaming about and will show you how you can earn 6 figures this year.

You'll experience the Rejuvenate community of like-minded practitioners and coaches who are also committed to making a difference in this world. This workshop is so crucial for you to attend that we have decided to provide you and a friend with a FULL SCHOLARSHIP as our guests.

See the following pages for more details about this offer to you.

Thank you for being a practitioner or coach who really wants to serve more people through your work. We're delighted to support you through what you've learned so far.

We wish you incredible success. And we hope to meet you in person soon.

Love and Success,

Jesse & Sharla

Jesse Koren and Sharla Jacobs

Special Bonus Offer

Attend Jesse and Sharla's
Rejuvenate Your Practice 2 Day Intensive
on FULL SCHOLARSHIP

As a thank-you for purchasing Sell is Not a 4-Letter Word, Jesse and Sharla are offering a FULL SCHOLARSHIP for you and a friend to attend the Rejuvenate Your Practice 2 Day Intensive as their complimentary guests. That's a total value of $1,994 – for free!   To assure your spot, please register immediately at www.RYPScholarship.com.

In only 2 Days you'll learn how to:

⦿ Have conversations so your potential clients **practically talk themselves into working with you** *(without being pushy)*

⦿ Feel completely natural talking with potential clients *(without nervousness or fear)*

⦿ Get over negative beliefs about how much you charge *(**over 50% of our participants raise their fees** and feel great about it)*

⦿ Use the **3 magic questions** when someone tells you, *'I can't afford it'* (people who say "No" to you because of money actually find a way to say **"Yes."**)

⦿ **Work with 5 simple fill-in-the-blank templates** for answering the question, *"What do you do?"* (so your potential clients are compelled to ask you more…)

⦿ And so much more!

Here's what other practitioners have said after attending the Rejuvenate Your Practice 2 Day Intensive…

Before I came to the Rejuvenate Your Practice™ 2 Day Intensive, I used to sit in my office and hope clients would miraculously come to me by referrals. If I did have a conversation with clients after they came, I would be so grateful that they trusted me and came to me, that I felt bad charging and would give them a huge discount on everything.

Then I took the Rejuvenate Your Practice™ 2 Day Intensive and I learned so much. I went from a 12' x 12' office and $1,800 per month to an office with four treatment rooms and between $8,000-9,000 per month in income."
-Cammi Montieth, ND, Steamboat Springs, CO

*"Within a few days of using this program, I got **5 new clients** from applying the principles, and it was easy and graceful. It's made such a difference in my attitude and manifested **lots of abundance** very quickly!"*
—Serina Chiba, Bodyworker

*"The Rejuvenate Your Practice™ 2 Day Intensive **totally shifted deeply ingrained negative attitudes** I have been holding for over 15 years. Now, I feel in true alignment with my personal sense of integrity when engaging in promoting my business… I finally feel able to be **compensated fully for my work**. Thank you! "*
— *Jessica Van Hulle, Spiritual Channel*

*"**Awesome seminar**. I have taken many chiropractic management courses and spent thousands of dollars. What you taught us this weekend… was **the most essential information**. Every [holistic practitioner] would benefit from what you have to teach."*
— Raphael Rettner, D.C

Claim Your **Full Scholarship** to the Rejuvenate Your Practice
2 Day Intensive www.RYPScholarship.com

REJUVENATE YOUR PRACTICE
2 DAY INTENSIVE
CERTIFICATE

Jesse Koren, Sharla Jacobs and Rejuvenate

Training invite you and a friend to attend

the Rejuvenate Your Practice 2 Day Intensive,

as complimentary guests. To register

and for more information go to

www.RYPScholarship.com

If you have no access to a computer,

call toll-free **1-800-632-2944 x100**

* This offer is open to all purchasers of Sell is Not a 4-Letter Word by Jesse Koren and Sharla Jacobs. Original proof of purchase is required. The offer is limited to the Rejuvenate Your Practice 2 Day Intensive weekend workshop only, and your registration in the workshop is subject to availability of space and/or changes to program schedule. This is a limited time offer. The value of this free admission for you and a friend is $1,994 as of December 2008. Organizations may not use more than one book to invite more than two people. While participants will be responsible for their travel and other costs, admission to the program is complimentary. Participants in the workshop are under no additional financial obligation whatsoever to Rejuvenate Training or Jesse Koren and Sharla Jacobs. Rejuvenate Training reserves the right to refuse admission to anyone it believes may disrupt the workshop, and to remove from the premises anyone it believes is disrupting the workshop.

Claim Your **Full Scholarship** to the Rejuvenate Your Practice
2 Day Intensive www.RYPScholarship.com

How to Share Heartselling™ with Colleagues and Friends

Often after learning about Heartselling™, we've found Holistic Practitioners and Coaches feel really inspired to share with their friends and colleagues about what they've learned. And it can be difficult to communicate the power of this new paradigm of selling when most practitioners and coaches feel resistant if not completely repelled by the notion of selling.

So we've found that the easiest way to share about Heartselling™ and Rejuvenate Training is to invite a friend to attend the Rejuvenate Your Practice 2 Day Intensive with you. You can invite them to purchase a book (or even buy one for them) to give them a head-start on the material, so when they attend the workshop, it will sink in on a deeper level.

We find that when you share with friends and colleagues about Heartselling, you're creating a community of like-minded practitioners and coaches who can support YOU in your vision to have a 6-Figure practice while you do the same.

And, when you invite friends to join you, you're rewarded by knowing you've made a difference in their lives and in the lives of the clients they will attract by virtue of their success.

Recommended Resources

Rejuvenate Training Programs

Rejuvenate Your Practice 2 Day Intensive – 2 Days

During the Rejuvenate Your Practice 2 Day Intensive you will learn the essential heart-based strategies to fill your practice for the rest of your life. You'll get the 5 Elements of Heartselling in your bones and your life and practice will never be the same.
www.RejuvenateYourPractice.com

Double Your Practice in 90 Days (or less) -90 Days

Most practitioners and coaches love working with clients, but have a hard time selling their services. The Double Your Practice in 90 Days Program gives you the tools and the support to do what you need to do in order to create a thriving practice in just 90 Days.
www.DoubleYourPractice.com

Leverage Your Genius Training Program – 5 months

At some point in your practice, trading your time for dollars and having a limit on your income no longer works for you. This exciting and inspiring program teaches you how to transform your practice into a profitable business where you work less and make more money. You'll learn how to increase the value you offer to your clients at the same time be able to work with more people. And you'll learn the 12 "Genius" strategies that support you to continually make a bigger difference.
www.LeverageYourGenius.com

Claim Your **Full Scholarship** to the Rejuvenate Your Practice
2 Day Intensive www.RYPScholarship.com

Build Your Empire Training Program – 5 months

The best place to have Heartselling™ conversations is at a workshop YOU are leading. In the Build Your Empire Program, we teach you everything you need to know to earn over $10,000 dollars in one weekend or $3,000 in a 90 minute class. Knowing these formulas gives you the ultimate security, because you'll know that as long as groups gather, you'll be successful. www.BuildYourEmpireProgram.com

Expand Your Empire Seminar – 4 Days

As you start leading workshops, you'll quickly find that the difference between a successful workshop and a not-so-successful workshop are actually subtle things that make a big difference. Join us for this amazing 4-Day seminar where we teach you the subtle things we've learned over the past 4 years that have made the difference between a $10,000 weekend and a $100,000 weekend.   www.ExpandYourEmpire.com

5 Elements for Living Women's Leadership Retreat Program – 12 months

Most women want to stand fully in their feminine power and create success in their business without compromising other aspects of life that matter most like family, friends and health. Unfortunately, most models of leadership revolve around masculine principles and don't utilize the beauty and wisdom of your feminine core. This amazing program helps you move beyond your fear and into a community of women who love you no matter what. You will be excited to meet your new self after 12 months of a deeper connection with yourself and the 5 Elements.   You'll learn business and leadership principles that will create success without burnout.
www.WomensLeadershipProgram.com

Claim Your **Full Scholarship** to the Rejuvenate Your Practice
2 Day Intensive www.RYPScholarship.com